MORPH-AID

A Source of Roots, Prefixes and Suffixes

Second Edition

Marilyn M. Toomey

CIRCUIT PUBLICATIONS

P.O. BOX 43072

CINCINNATI, OHIO 45243

ISBN: 0-923573-03-8

123456-TS-432109

Printed in the United States of America.

Table of Contents

Preface

Our first experiences assimilating word parts to form words, or breaking words down into smaller units of meaning probably occur in the early primary grades. From this time, our ability to detect word meaning by analyzing components and to form complex words by adding components develops. These skills continue to enable us to comprehend and express spoken and written language as our language ability grows.

Speakers and writers addressing students, even in early grades, assume that these skills are intact, and that students are, indeed, able to build words and decipher meaning by this means. Many language arts materials offer exercises for advancing students' ability to use these principles of word analysis as their language develops. Often, vocabulary-building exercises are based on these assumptions.

When a student's language is not developing as expected, the concept of word analysis and word building might not be serving him or her as one might assume. This student might need specific, direct instruction in order to understand how word roots, prefixes, and suffixes function in our language.

Teaching these skills can be rewarding because we know that we are helping a student to develop an important tool for language learning. On the other hand, preparing lessons to meet this goal can be frustrating because of the tedious and time-consuming efforts necessary to find examples of words containing particular roots and affixes, and to prepare presentation and practice material. *Morph-Aid* will save you much time in preparing such lessons.

The contents of this book are divided into two parts, Resource Lists and Support Materials. The first part, the Resource Lists, are lists of roots, prefixes, suffixes and their definitions, each followed by examples of words containing the respective affix or morpheme.

The second part of the book, Support Materials, is intended to support your efforts in teaching how affixes or morphemes change word meanings.

Thirty-three pages are devoted to specific prefixes and suffixes. Each of these pages offers the particular prefix or suffix (or contrasting pair or group) defined, utilized as derivatives, and then used in context. These pages might be used as a means of presenting or teaching the target affix or morpheme and are, therefore, referred to as Presentation Pages. On the page opposite each of the Presentation Pages is a Writing Worksheet which is meant to strengthen the presentation and discussion using written exercises. Here, the student reviews definitions, divides derivatives into roots and affixes, composes and writes original sentences, and answers questions found on the Presentation Page.

Please note that the term *derivative* is freely used on the Presentaton Pages and Writing Worksheets. Though this term might be unfamiliar to some of your students, it is a useful word occurring in classroom materials as well as information media. I generally find that teaching the meaning and use of the word *derivative* is effort well spent. Actually, such a lesson might *introduce* your students to the notion of combining a root word with an affix to form a new word.

Finally, Activity Pages and Crossword Puzzles are offered for further expansion of selected affixes and target words. Randomly presented, these exercises challenge students to utilize these words in context.

I hope that *Morph-Aid* will prove to be a helpful addition to your reference collection and that you and your students share some enjoyable moments working with these materials.

Roots

A root is that part of a word expressing its basic meaning. It can occur in any word position. Spelling might vary slightly since some roots have their origins in non-English words.

ac -- do

action	interaction
active	manufacture
activity	practical
actor	practice
actress	practicum
actually	react
actuate	reaction
counteract	reenact
deactivate	retroactive
inactive	transact

aero -- air

aerobic	aeronaut
aerodynamic	aeronautic
aerodyne	aerosol
aerology	aerospace
aeromechanics	anaerobic
aeromedicine	

agr -- farm

agrarian	agricultural
agribusiness	agriculture

alt -- high

altimeter	exaltation
altitude	exalted
exalt	unexalted

ambi -- both ways

ambidextrous	ambiguous
ambience	ambivalence
ambient	ambivalent
ambiguities	ambiance

ami -- friend

amiable	amigo
amiably	amity
amicable	

amo -- love

amorist	gamete
amorous	heterogamous
bigamy	monogamy
enamor	paramour
endogamous	polygamy
exogamous	

amphi -- both ways

amphibian	amphipod
amphibious	amphitheater

ang -- bend

angle	rectangle
angular	triangle

anim -- feeling

animation	animosity
animism	animus

ann -- year

annals	per annum
annual	semiannual
annuity	

apt -- suitable

adapt	adapter
adaptation	aptitude

aqua -- water

aquamarine	aquarium
aquanaut	aquatic

arch -- main, highest

anarchist
anarchy
archbishop
hierarchy

matriarch
monarch
oligarchy
patriarch

art -- skill

artifact
artifice
artificial

artisan
artist
artistic

aud -- hear

audible
audience
audio
audiology

audio-visual
audition
auditory
inaudible

auto -- self

autobiography
autocrat
autograph
automatic
automation

automobile
autonomy
autopilot
autopsy

bene -- good

benediction
benefactor
beneficial

beneficent
benefit
benevolent

bio -- life

amphibious
biochemistry
biologist

biology
biopsy
symbiotic

cap -- head

capital
capitulate
capsize

captain
caption
decapitate

card -- heart

cardiac
cardinal
cardiology

cardiovascular
electrocardiogram
myocardium

cas -- box, chest or container

bookcase
briefcase
casement
casing
casket

cassette
encase
showcase
staircase
suitcase

cede -- go

accede
antecedent
concede
exceed
exceedingly
intercede

precede
precedent
proceed
recede
secede
succeed

ceive -- to take

conceive
deceive
perceive

receipt
receive

cent -- one hundred

centennial
centimeter
centipede
cents

century
percent
percentile

cent -- center

adjacent
centered
centerpiece
central
centrifugal

centrifuge
concentric
decentralize
eccentric
egocentric

cept -- take

accept
concept
contraceptive
except
intercept

misconception
perception
reception
receptor
susceptible

chron -- time

anachronism
chronic
chronicle
chronological

chronology
diachronic
synchronize

cide -- cut, kill

decide	infanticide
genocide	matricide
germicide	patricide
herbicide	pesticide
homicide	suicide

cine -- move

cinema	cinematographer
cinematic	cinematography

circ -- around

circle	circumscribe
circuit	circumstance
circulate	circumvent
circumference	circus
circumnavigate	encircle

cis -- cut, kill

circumcise	incision
concise	incisor
decision	precise
decisive	scissors
excise	

clam (claim) -- shout

acclaim	proclaim
clamor	proclamation
counterclaim	reclaim
disclaim	reclamation
exclaim	unclaimed
exclamation	

clar -- clear

clarification	declaration
clarify	declare
clarify	undeclared
clear	

cline -- lean

decline	inclined
inclination	recline
incline	

clos -- shut

cloister	disclose
close	foreclose
closet	

clud -- shut

conclude	occluded
exclude	preclude
include	seclusion

clus -- shut

claustrophobia	inconclusive
cluster	malocclusion
conclusion	recluse
exclusive	

cogn -- know

cognizance	incognito
cognition	recognize
cognitive	recognition

contr -- against

contraband	contrast
contradict	contravene
contrary	controversy

cord -- heart, mind

accord	cordial
accords	discord
concordance	record

corp -- body

corporal	corpse
corporate	corpulent
corporation	corpuscle
corps	incorporate

crat -- power, rule

aristocrat	democracy
autocracy	Dixiecrat
bureaucrat	technocrat

cred -- believe

accredited	creditors
credence	credo
credentials	discredit
credibility	incredible
credit	incredulous

cur -- run

concurrent	incur
current	occur
courier	precursor
excursion	recurrent

cycle -- wheel

bicycle	cyclorama
cycle	encyclical
cyclometer	encyclopedia
cyclone	tricycle
Cyclops	unicycle

derm -- skin

dermal	hypodermic
dermis	pachyderm
epidermis	taxidermy

dict -- speak, point out in words

benediction	indict
contradict	jurisdiction
dictator	predict
diction	valedictorian
dictionary	vindictive
edict	

duct -- lead

abduct	induction
adduct	seduction
aqueduct	semiconductor
conductor	viaduct

equ -- equal

equation	equity
equator	equivocal
equidistant	inequality
equilibrium	inequity
equinox	unequivocally
equitable	

fac -- make, do

artifact	factor
fact	factory
facetious	

fec -- make, do

confection	effective
confectionery	infect
defect	perfect
defective	perfection
disinfectant	refect
effect	refectory

fer -- carry, bear

afferent	offer
confer	offering
conference	prefer
differ	preferred
different	refer
ferret	referee
ferry	transfer

fic -- pretend

fictitious	fictive
fiction	nonfiction

fid -- faithful

confident	fiduciary
diffidence	infidel
fidelity	perfidy

firm -- fixed

affirm	confirmation
affirmative	infirm
confirm	infirmary

flect -- bend

deflect	inflection
genuflect	reflect
inflect	reflection

flex -- bend

flexible	flexuous
flexion	reflexes
flexor	reflexive

form -- shape

conform	formula
cuneiform	informal
deform	malformed
deformity	nonconformist
formal	reform
formant	transform
format	uniform
formation	waveform
forms	

fract -- break

fraction	fractus
fractional	fracas
fracture	infraction

frag -- break

fragile	fragmentary
fragment	fragmentate

fund -- bottom, base

fundamental	profound
funds	profundity

fus -- pour

confuse	infuse
diffuse	profusely
fuse	transfusion

gam -- marriage

bigamy	monogamy
exogamy	polygamy
gamete	

gen -- kind, class, race, birth

congenital	genocide
degenerate	genotype
engendered	genre
eugenic	genus
gender	generous
genealogy	heterogenous
general	homogeneous
generation	regenerate
generic	

geo -- earth

geocentric	geometry
geography	geomorphology
geology	geophysics

grad -- step

degrade	gradual
downgrade	graduate
grade	graduation
gradient	upgrade

graph -- write, record

bibliography	mimeograph
choreographer	monograph
cryptographic	oceanographic
electrocardiograph	orthography
epigraph	paragraph
graphic	phonograph
lexicography	spectrograph
lithograph	typographical

grat -- pleasing

grateful	gratuity
gratification	ingratitude
gratify	grateful
gratitude	

greg -- group

aggregate	egregious
congregate	gregarious
congregation	segregate
desegregate	

gress -- step

aggressive
digress
progress

progressive
regress
transgress

hab -- have, hold

habile
habit
habitant
habitat

habitual
inhabit
rehabilitate

hosp -- host

hospice
hospital
hospitable

hospitality
inhospitable

init -- beginning

initial
initiate

initiation
initiative

ject -- throw

abject
conjecture
deject
eject
inject
injection

interject
object
project
reject
trajectory

jud -- law, right

adjudicate
judge
judgment
judiciary

judicious
misjudge
prejudice

junct -- join

adjunct
conjunction
disjunct
injunction

junction
juncture
subjunctive

jur -- law, right

abjure
jurisdiction
jurisprudence

juror
jury

jus -- law, right

adjust
injustice
just
justice

justify
justly
unjust

kine -- move

kinescope
kinesiology
kinesthesia

kinesthetic
kinetic

lab -- work

belabor
collaborate
elaborate

labor
laboratory
laborer

lat -- carry, lift

circulate
collate
correlate
elate
escalate

ovulate
relative
tabulate
translate
ventilate

lev -- raise

elevate
elevation
elevator
levee

level
lever
levitate
levity

lib -- free

ad-lib
filibuster
liberal

liberate
liberation
liberty

loc -- place

allocate
dislocate
local
locale
location
locomotion
locomotive
relocate

loc (loq) -- speak

circumlocution
colloquial
colloquialism
colloquium
elocution
eloquent
locution
loquacious
loquacity

log -- word

analogy
analogy
anthology
apology
catalog
dialogist
dialogue
epilogue
eulogy
logic
logical
logo
monologue
prologue
syllogism

luc -- bright, light

elucidate
hallucinate
lucent
lucerne
lucid
translucent

lum -- bright, light

illuminate
luminario
luminous
photoluminescence

luna -- moon

lunacy
lunar
lunatic
sublunary
superlunary

lus -- bright, light

illustrate
lackluster
luster
lustrous

mag -- great

magistrate
magnanimous
magnate
magnificent
magnify
magnitude

mal -- bad

malady
malaise
malaria
malice
malicious
malign

man -- hand

dismantle
emancipate
maneuver
manipulate
manual
manufacture
manuscript
penmanship

mand -- order

command
commandment
commando
demand
mandate
remand
reprimand

mar -- sea

aquamarine
marinated
marine
mariner
maritime
marooned
marsh
submarine
submariner

mater -- mother

maternal
maternity
matriarch
matricide
matron
matronly

mech -- machine

machine
mechanic
mechanical
mechanization
mechanize

---

med -- middle

immediate
intermediary
intermediate
medial
median

mediate
mediocre
mediterranean
medium

mem -- mindful

commemorate
immemorial
memento
memo
memoir

memorabilia
memorandum
memorial
memory
remember

merg -- dip, dive

emerge
emergency
emergent

merge
merger
submerge

meter -- measure

centimeter
kilometer
metric
metrics
metrist
metrology

metrology
metronome
parameter
pentameter
pyrometer

micro -- small

microbe
microcomputer
microcosm
microfilm
micron

microphone
microscope
microscopic
microwave

mid -- middle

amid
amidst
midair
midday
middle

midland
midnight
midshipman
midwestern

min -- less, to lessen

diminish
diminution
miniature

minimum
minority
minus

mis -- send

admission
commissary
dismiss
emissary
emission
missile

mission
omission
promise
remission
submissive

mit -- send

admit
commit
commit
emit

omit
permit
remit
submit

mono -- one

carbon monoxide
monarch
monogamy
monograph
monolith

monologue
monopoly
monorail
monotheism
monotony

mor -- death

immortal
morbid
morgue
moribund

mortal
mortician
mortify
rigormortis

morph -- shape, form

amorphous
anthropomorphic
geomorphology

metamorphosis
morpheme
morphemics

mot -- move

demote
emotion
motel
motion
motivation

motor
motorcycle
osmosis
remote

mov -- move

immovable
movable
movement

movie
moving
remove

multi -- many

multicolored
multiple
multiply
multipurpose
multitude

mut -- change

commute
mutants
mutation
mutual
permutation
transmutation

nat -- born

innate
nation
native
nativity
nature
neonatal

naut -- sailor

aeronautics
Argonaut
astronaut
cosmonaut
nautical
nautilus

nav -- ship

circumnavigate
naval
navigate
navigator
navy
unnavigable

neg -- deny, not

abnegate
negate
negation
negative
neglect
negligible
negotiate
renegade
renege

nom -- name

anonymous
denomination
ignominy
nomenclature
nominally
nominate
nominative
nominee

not -- mark

annotated
banknote
connotation
denotation
footnote
keynote
notable
notary
notation
note
notebook
noteworthy
notice
notify
notoriety
notorious

noun -- announce

announce
announcement
denounce
mispronounce
pronounce
renounce

nov -- new

innovative
nova
novel
novelty
novice
novitiate
renovate

numer -- number

enumerate
innumerable
number
numeral
numeric
numerical
numerology
numerous

nunc -- announce

annunciation
enunciate
nuncio
pronunciation
renounce

ocu -- eye

binoculars
focus
innocuous
monocle
ocular
oculist

opt -- eye

optic
optical
optician
optics
optometrist
optometry

ord -- row

coordinate
extraordinary
ordain
order
orderly

ordinal
ordinance
ordinary
ordinate
primordial

orig -- begin

aboriginal
aborigine
origin

original
originate
unoriginal

orth -- straight

orthodontist
orthodox
orthography

orthopedic
unorthodox

pan -- all

expand
panacea

pandemonium
panorama

para -- beside, equal

compare
disparity
incomparable
parable
parachute
paradigm
paradox

parallel
paralyze
parameter
paranoid
paraphrase
parasite
paratrooper

pater -- father

compatriot
paternal
paternity
patriarch

patriot
patron
patronage

path -- suffering

apathy
empathy
pathetic
pathological

pathology
pathos
sympathetic
sympathy

ped -- foot

biped
centipede
expedient
expedite
impede
impediment
moped
orthopedic
pedal

pedestal
pedestrian
pedicel
pedicure
pedigree
pediment
peduncle
quadruped

pel -- push

compel
dispel
expel
impel

pellet
propel
repel
repellent

pend -- hang

append
appendage
appendix
depend
expend
impend
independent

pendant
pending
pendulous
pendulum
perpendicular
suspenders
suspending

peri -- around

pericardium
pericline
pericycle
perigee
perimeter

period
periodically
peripheral
periphery
periscope

phil -- love

philander
philanthropy
philharmonic
philodendron

philology
philosopher
philosophy

phon -- sound

allophone
cacophony
earphones
gramophone
headphones
homophone
megaphone
microphone
monophonic
phoneme
phonetic
phonograph
phonology
saxophone
stereophonic
symphony
telephone
vibraphone

photo -- light

photocathode
photocopy
photoelectric
photogenic
photograph
photon
photosensitive
photosynthesis
telephoto

phys -- nature

astrophysics
biophysics
geophysics
physical
physician
physicist
physics
physiognomy
physiology
physique

plex -- intertwining, network

apoplexy
complex
complexion
complexity
multiplex
perplexed
plexus

plic -- fold, interwoven

complicate
complication
implications
implicit
replica

plur -- more

plural
pluralism
plurality
pluralize

pod -- foot

brachiopod
podiatry
podium
tripod

polis -- city

acropolis
heliopolis
megalopolis
metropolis

polit -- city

cosmopolitan
metropolitan
political
politics

poly -- many

monopoly
polyandry
polychromatic
polyester
polyethylene
polygamy
polygraph
polymer
polynomial
polyunsaturated

pop -- people

overpopulated
pops
populace
popular
population
unpopular

port -- carry

comport
deport
export
import
passport
portable
portage
portal
portend
portfolio
purport
rapport
report
support
transport
transportation

pos -- place, put

apostle
compose
composite
depose
deposit
expose
impose
juxtaposed
oppose
opposite
pose
position
positive
predisposed
propose
superimpose
transposed

post -- after

posthumously	postpone
postmortem	postscript
postpaid	postwar

prehend -- seize

apprehend	prehensile
comprehend	reprehend
comprehension	reprehensible

prim -- first

premier	prime
prima	prime minister
primacy	primer
primary	primeval
primate	primitive

princ -- first

prince	principal
princess	principality

psych -- mind, soul

neuropsychiatry	psychoanalysis
parapsychology	psychology
psyche	psychopath
psychedelic	psychosis
psychiatry	psychotic

pugn -- fight

impugn	pugnacious
pugilist	repugnant
pugilistic	

puls -- push

compulsive	pulsar
compulsory	pulsate
expulsive	pulse
impulsive	repulsive
propulsion	

put -- reckon, count, consider

compute	impute
computer	reputation
deputy	repute
dispute	

quer -- seek, search

conquer	inquire
enquire	query

ques -- seek, search

conquest	question
quest	request

quis -- seek, search

acquisitive	quiz
conquistador	relinquish
exquisite	requisition
inquisition	vanquish

rad -- root, ray

eradicate	radiation
irradiate	radical
radar	radio
radial	radius
radiant	rays
radiate	

rect -- straight

correct	rectangle
direction	rectify
erect	rectitude
indirect	

reg -- king

foreign	regiment
regal	region
regale	regnal
regalia	regular
regency	regulate
regent	regulation
regicide	reign

rid (ris) -- laugh

deride
derisive
riddle
ridicule
ridiculous
risibility
risible

rogat -- ask, claim

abrogate
arrogate
derogate
interrogate
interrogative
prerogative
rogue
surrogate

rupt -- break

abrupt
bankrupt
corrupt
disrupt
erupt
interrupt
irrupt
rupture

san -- healthy, clean

insane
sanatorium
sane
sanguine
sanitary
unsanitary

sanc -- saint

sanctify
sanctimonious
sanction
sanctuary

scend -- climb

ascend
condescend
crescendo
descend
transcend
transcendental

sci -- know

conscious
disciple
discipline
omniscient
science
scientist
subconscious

sci -- cut, distinguish

abscissa
rescind
schism
schist

script -- write

circumscription
description
inscription
manuscript
postscript
prescription
scripture
subscription
transcription

sec -- cut, set apart

bisect
consecutive
desecrate
dissect
insect
intersect
secede
seclude
secret
sect
section
sector
secular
secure
trisect
vivisect

sed (sid) -- remain

residue
sedate
sedentary
sediment
sedimentation

sens -- feelings

desensitize
sensation
sensational
sense
sensitive
sensor
sensory
sensual
sensuous

sent -- thought

consent
dissent
resent
sentence
sentient
sentimental
sentinel

sequ -- follow

consequence
inconsequential
obsequious
sequel
sequence
sequential
sequester
subsequent

---

serv -- help, watch over

conservation
conservative
conserve
deserve
disservice
observe
preserve

reserve
servant
service
serviceman
servile
servitude
subservient

set -- remain

beset
inset
offset
onset
reset
setback

settle
settlement
settler
sunset
upset

sign -- mark

assign
assignment
consign
design
designate
ensign
insignia

resign
sign
signal
signature
significant
signify

sim -- like

assimilate
dissimilar
facsimile

similar
simulate
simultaneous

sist -- stand

assist
consist
consistency
insist
persist

persistent
resist
subsist
subsistence

sol -- alone

isolate
solace
sole

solitary
solitude
solo

solu -- loosen

absolute
dissolution
insoluble
resolve

soldering
soluble
solution

solv -- loosen

dissolve
insolvent
resolve

solve
solvency
solvent

son -- sound

consonant
dissonant
resonance

sonar
sonata
sonorous

spec -- see

circumspect
inspect
introspective
perspective
prospect
retrospect

speck
spectacular
spectrogram
spectrum
suspect

spic -- see

auspices
conspicuous
perspicacious

perspicuous
suspicion

spir -- breath, spirit

aspirate
aspire
conspire
inspire
perspire

respiration
respirator
spirited
spiritual
transpire

stat -- stand, standing

state
statement
static
station
stationary
statistics

statuary
statue
statuette
status
status quo
statutory

stimu -- whip, agitate

stimulable	stimulation
stimulate	stimulus

strict -- tight, tighten

constrict	restriction
constricting	striction
restrict	stricture

struct -- build

construction	instruct
destruction	obstruct
indestructible	structure

sup -- superior, highest

insuperable	supersede
super	supersonic
superimpose	superstar
superiority	support
supernal	supreme
supernatural	unsupervised

tact -- touch

contact	tactile
intact	tactless
tactful	tactual

tang -- touch

cotangent	tangent
intangible	tangible

temp -- time

contemporary	temperate
extemporaneous	tempo
temper	temporal
temperance	temporary

ten -- hold, stretch

contend	tentacle
tenacious	tentative
tenacity	tenuous
tense	tenuously
tension	tenure

term -- end

determine	predetermined
exterminate	terminal
interminable	terminate

terr -- land, earth

extraterrestrial	terrarium
subterranean	terrestrial
terrace	terrier
terrain	territory

theo -- god

apotheosis	pantheon
apotheosize	polytheism
atheism	theology
monotheism	

thermo -- heat

thermal	thermonuclear
thermocouple	thermos
thermodynamics	thermostat
thermometer	

tort -- twist

contortion	retort
distortion	torte
extorting	tortilla
extortionist	torture

tract -- pull, draw

abstract	retract
attract	subtract
contract	tract
detract	tractable
distract	traction
extract	tractor
protractor	

trans -- across

intransigent	transit
intransitive	transition
transact	translate
transcend	transmit
transcribe	transparent
transfer	transpire
transform	transport
transient	transvestite

trib -- give

attribute	retribution
contribute	tributary
distribute	tribute

trud -- push

extrude	obtrude
intrude	protrude

trus -- push

extrusion	protrusion
intrusion	unobtrusive

turb -- confuse, stir up

disturbance	turbojet
perturb	turboprop
turbid	turbulence
turbine	turbulent
turbo	turmoil

vag -- wander

vagabond	vagrant
vagrancy	vague

var -- different

invariably	varicose
variable	varied
variance	variegated
variant	variety
variation	various
varicolored	vary

ven -- come

advent	event
adventure	eventually
avenue	invent
circumvent	inventive
convene	prevent
convent	reconvene
convention	venture

vers -- turn

adverse	obverse
aversion	reverse
controversy	subversive
conversation	universal
converse	versatile
diverse	version
diversity	versus
inversion	vise versa

vert -- turn

avert	invert
controvert	pervert
convert	revert
convertible	subvert
divert	vertex
extrovert	vertigo
introvert	

vict -- conquer

convict	victor
evict	victorious
victim	victory

vis -- see

invisible	vision
television	visionary
visa	visit
visage	visor
visible	vista

viv -- live

convivial	vivacious
revive	vivacity
survive	vivid

voc -- voice

advocate	revoke
evoke	unequivocal
invocation	vocabulary
invoke	vocal
irrevocable	vocalist
nonvocal	vocative
provocative	vociferous
provoke	

volv -- roll

convoluted	revolutionary
evolve	revolve
involve	revolver

Prefixes

A prefix is a morpheme that alters the meaning of a word when joined to the beginning of the word.

a -- not, away from

achromatic	aphasia
agraphia	aphyllous
amentia	apraxia
amoral	asymmetry
amorphous	asynchronism
apathetic	ataxia
aperture	avert

ab -- away from

abdicate	ablactation
abjure	abnormal

ac -- to, toward

accede	accolade
accelerate	acquire

ad -- toward

addict	adduce
addictive	adduction
address	adductor

ana -- back, again

Anabaptist	anapest
anachronism	anaplastic
anagram	anastomosis

ante -- before

antebellum	antemeridian
antecedent	antemortem
antechamber	antenatal
antedate	antetype

anti -- against

antiaircraft	antilithic
antibacterial	antimagnetic
antibody	antimaterialistic
anticlerical	antimissile
anticlimax	antipode
anticlinal	antiseptic
anticoagulant	antithesis
antigen	antitoxin
antilabor	antitrust

apo -- from, away

apocrine	apology
apocrypha	apoplexy
apogee	apostrophe

arch -- chief, first

archangel	archdiocese
archbishop	archduchess
archdeacon	archduke

bi -- two

biangular	bimanual
biathlon	bimonthly
bicentennial	binary
biceps	binaural
bicuspid	binocular
bicycle	binomial
biennial	biplane
bifid	bipod
bifocal	biracial
bifoliate	bisect
bifurcate	bivalve
bigeneric	biweekly

cata -- down

cataclysm	catastrophe
catapult	catatonic
catastasis	

circum -- around

circumference	circumscribe
circumflex	circumspect
circumlocution	circumstance
circumnavigate	circumvallate
circumrotate	circumvolve

cis -- on this side

cisalpine	cislunar
cisatlantic	

co -- with, along or together with

coauthor	cohabit
codefendant	coincide
coeducational	coinsurance
coefficient	cooperate
coexist	coordinate
coextend	

contra -- against

contraception	contrapositive
contradict	contrapuntal
contraindicate	contravallation

counter -- against

counteract	counterforce
counterattack	counterinsurgency
counterbalance	counterintelligence
counterblow	countermand
countercharge	countermarch
counterclaim	countermeasure
counterclockwise	counterpoint
counterfeit	counterproductive

de -- do the opposite of

deactivate	deemphasize
debark	defame
debase	defuse
debug	denature
decaffeinated	depreciate
decapitate	derail
decentralize	desegregate
decompose	desensitize
decontrol	detoxify
deduce	devalue

di -- two, twice

diacid	dihybrid
diatomic	dioxide
dicephalous	diphase
digraph	

dia -- across, through

diachronic	diagonal
diacritic	diagram
diagenesis	diameter

dia -- between, away

diagnosis	dialogue
dialect	diaphragm

dis -- not, without

disable
disaccord
disadvantage
disagree
disallow
disassemble
disclaim
discolor
disconnect
discontent
discredit
disgrace
disjoin
dislike
disloyal
disobey
displease
disregard
disrespect
disunity

dys -- bad

dysentery
dysgenic
dyslexic
dysphasia
dysphonia
dystrophy

en -- make, cause to be, put in the state of

enable
encircle
enclose
encounter
encumber
endear
enlarge
enrich
enshrine
entangle

epi -- on, outside

epicanthus
epicenter
epidermis
epiglottis
epigraph
epitaph
epithelium

equi -- equal

equidistant
equilateral
equilibrium
equinox
equipoise
equipotential
equivocal

eu -- good

eugenic
eulogy
euphemism
euphonic
euphoria
euphrasy

ex -- out

excavate
exceed
exclude
excommunicate
exocrine
exodus
exogamy
exoskeleton
expand
expire
export
extrude

extra -- beyond

extracorporeal
extralegal
extramarital
extramural
extraordinary
extraplanetary
extrasensory
extraterrestrial
extravascular

fore -- front, before

forebrain
foreground
forehead
foreleg
forelock
forename
forenoon
foreshadow
foresight
foretell

hyper -- beyond, over

hyperactive
hyperbola
hypercharge
hyperkinetic
hypermetric
hypersensitive
hypersonic
hypertension
hypertonic
hyperventilate

hypo -- under, less

hypodermic
hypoglycemia
hypokinesis
hypoplasia
hypotension
hypothalamus
hypothermal
hypotonic

il -- not

illegitimate
illiquid
illiterate
illogical

im -- in

imbibe	imperil
immigrate	implant
impacted	implode
impanel	impose
impart	impoverish
impel	impress

im -- not

immodest	imperceptible
immoral	imperfect
immortal	imperturbable
immobile	impolite
immovable	imponderable
impartial	impossible
impassible	improper
impatient	imprudent
impeccable	impure

in -- in

inboard	inhume
inborn	inject
inbred	inject
incarcerate	inland
income	inlay
incorporate	inmate
incubate	inmost
indebted	inoculate
induce	input
infield	inquire
infuse	inscribe
inhabit	inseminate
inhale	insert
inherent	intake
in-house	invade

in -- not

inappropriate	incorrect
inarticulate	independent
inattentive	indivisible
incalculable	inept
incapable	inequality
inclement	infertile
incognito	injustice
incompetent	insolvent
incomprehensible	intolerable
inconsistent	invisible

inter -- among, between

interchange	interlunar
intercom	international
intercommunicate	interpersonal
intercontinental	interplanetary
interdenominational	interregnum
interfaith	interstate
interlude	

intra -- within

intracellular	intraspecific
intracoastal	intrastate
intradermal	intrauterine
intramolecular	intravenous
intramural	intrazonal

intro -- inside

introduce	introspection
intromit	introvert
introspect	

mal -- bad, improper

maladaptation	malformation
maladjusted	malfunction
maladroit	malocclusion
malaise	malodorous
malevolence	

meta -- change

metachromatism	metaphase
metamorphous	metaphor

meta -- going beyond

metalinguistic	metaphysical
metamathematics	metapsychology

mis -- wrong

misconduct	mismatch
misconstrue	misnomer
misfile	misplace
misfit	misprint
misguide	mispronounce
mishandle	misquote
misinform	misread
misinterpret	misrepresent
misjudge	misspeak
mislabel	misspell
mislaid	mistake
mislead	mistrust
mismanage	misuse

mono -- one

monochromatic	monomorphic
monocle	monoplane
monoculture	monoplegia
monocyte	monosyllabic
monogenesis	monotheism
monogram	monotone
monolingual	monotype

neo -- new

Neo-Latin	neolithic
neoclassic	neonatal
neocolonialism	neoplasm
neogenesis	

non -- not, opposite of

nonabsorbent	nondecaying
nonaddictive	nondefensive
nonadjustable	nonmalignant
nonaggressive	nonmember
nonalcoholic	nonperforming
noncombat	nonperishable
nonconformist	nonprofessional
nonconnective	nontoxic
nonconsent	nonverbal
noncurrent	nonvisual

ob -- to, toward

obdurate	obstinate
obfuscate	obstruct
obscure	obtrusive
obsequious	obverse

para -- beside, compared to

parable	paraprofessional
parachute	parapsychology
paradox	parasite
paralegal	parasympathetic
paramedical	parathyroid

per -- throughout

perceive	permutation
percolate	perplex
perfume	

peri -- around

pericardium	perimorph
perigee	periscope
perimeter	peristalsis

poly -- many

polychromatic	polymorph
polycyclic	polynomial
polydactyl	polyphase
polyelectrolyte	polysyllabic
polyethylene	polytechnic
polyhedron	polytheism

post -- after

postdate	postpaid
postgraduate	postpartum
posthumous	postpone
posthypnotic	postscript
postoperative	postwar

pre -- before

prearrange	premeditate
precancel	prenatal
precaution	prerevolutionary
precede	preschool
precept	preseason
precursor	pretest
preface	pretrial
prefix	preview
preheat	prewar
prejudice	prewashed

re -- again

reclassify	refill
recombine	refire
recompute	refurnish
recopy	regrind
redecorate	relocate
rededicate	relock
redefine	remix
redeliver	reopen
redesign	reorder
rediscover	resell
reexplain	retell
refashion	rewrite

retro -- backward

retroactive	retrogress
retrocede	retrospect
retroflex	

semi -- half, partial

semiannual	semiformal
semicircle	semiliquid
semidarkness	semiprofessional
semifinal	semitransparent

sub -- below, beneath, a smaller amount, less important

subclass	subheading
subcompact	subliminal
subconscious	submarine
subcontract	subtopic
subgroup	suburb

super -- above, over, beyond

supereminent	supernatural
superficial	supernumerary
superfine	supersede
superhuman	supersonic
superimpose	superstar

sur -- above, over

surpass	surround
surplus	surtax
surrealism	surveilance

sym -- together, with

symbiosis	symphony
symmetry	symposium
sympathy	symptom

syn -- together, with

synchronize	synod
syncopate	synopsis
syndrome	syntax
synergetic	synthesis

tele -- far

telegram	telephoto
telegraph	teleprompter
telekinesis	telescope
telemeter	teletype
telephone	television

trans -- across, over, through

transatlantic	transmigrant
transcend	transmit
transcontinental	transoceanic
transcribe	transpacific
transfer	transparent
transfix	transpire
transform	transplant
transfuse	transport
transgress	transpose
transilient	transsexual
translucent	transude
transmarine	transverse

tri -- three

triangle	trifocal
triarchy	triform
tribasic	trilingual
triceps	triplane
tricolor	triplex
tricuspid	tripod

ultra -- beyond

ultraconservative	ultrared
ultrahigh	ultrasensitive
ultramarine	ultrasonic
ultramodern	ultraviolet

un -- not, opposite of

unacceptable	unethical
unaffiliated	unexpected
unafraid	unhappy
unambiguous	unhurt
unamusing	uninvited
unassigned	unopened
unbelievable	unpopular
unclaimed	unsigned
undefeated	unsold
undeveloped	unsuccessful

uni -- one

uniaxial	unidimensional
unicellular	unidirectional
unicorn	uniform
unicostate	unilateral
unicycle	univalve

up -- up

upbeat	upright
upbringing	uproot
update	upshot
upgrade	upstairs
uphill	upstream
uphold	upswing
upkeep	uptown
uplift	upturn
upmost	upward

Suffixes

A suffix is a morpheme which changes the meaning of a word when added to the end of the word.

able -- tending to, fit for

achievable	noticeable
admirable	objectionable
amenable	payable
believable	portable
changeable	predictable
comfortable	profitable
comparable	questionable
curable	reasonable
disposable	removable
educable	returnable
enjoyable	sinkable
erasable	solvable
fashionable	suitable
forgettable	taxable
honorable	tolerable
manageable	usable
movable	variable
negotiable	washable

acious -- inclined to

fallacious	tenacious
pugnacious	voracious
sagacious	

ade -- result of action, person involved in an action

accolade	decade
balustrade	escapade
barricade	lemonade
blockade	limeade
brigade	marinade
brocade	marmalade
cavalcade	masquerade
colonnade	promenade
comrade	renegade

age -- amount, collection of

acreage
baggage
carnage
coinage
dosage
drainage
footage
herbage
leakage
leverage
linkage
luggage
mileage
patronage
percentage
roughage
seepage
sewage
shrinkage
wattage
wreckage

aire -- connected, associated with

billionaire
concessionaire
doctrinaire
millionaire
questionnaire
solitaire

al -- relating to

abdominal
accidental
agricultural
bilingual
biological
brutal
causal
central
classical
clinical
coastal
coincidental
comical
commercial
congressional
corporal
identical
informational
logical
naval
nocturnal
normal
physical
practical
promotional
regal
rental
skeletal
social
spinal
survival
tonal
tropical
vocal

ance -- quality, state of

abeyance
accordance
allowance
assurance
attendance
clearance
compliance
defiance
deviance
dominance
entrance
fragrance
importance
petulance
reliance
remembrance
resonance
riddance
variance
vigilance

ant -- something which or someone who performs an action

accountant
applicant
combatant
informant
migrant
occupant
pollutant
registrant
servant
tyrant

ar -- one who

beggar
consular
registrar
scholar

ary -- connected with, pertaining to

hereditary
honorary
imaginary
incendiary
judiciary
military
missionary
momentary
monetary
necessary
parliamentary
planetary
primary
sanitary
supplementary
voluntary

archy -- ruling, that which is ruled

matriarchy
monarchy
oligarchy
patriarchy

ard -- one who performs an action or has some quality to greater than expected degree

drunkard
laggard
sluggard
wizard

arian -- involved with, characterized by

authoritarian
barbarian
grammarian
humanitarian
librarian
nonagenarian
octogenarian
sectarian
seminarian
totalitarian
vegetarian
veterinarian

ate -- of, having to do with

abbreviate	dominate
antiquate	duplicate
assassinate	equate
authenticate	formulate
calculate	intoxicate
collegiate	literate
congregate	mandate
contaminate	populate
decapitate	radiate
dictate	salivate
doctorate	syllabicate
domesticate	ulcerate

bound -- limited to, surrounded by, caught in

clothbound	rock-bound
eastbound	southbound
homebound	spellbound
inbound	stormbound
northbound	westbound
outbound	

cle -- small

icicle	tubercle
particle	

craft -- skill, craft, product of skill or craft

handicraft	witchcraft
leathercraft	woodcraft
stagecraft	

cy -- state of being

accuracy	dormancy
adequacy	flagrancy
buoyancy	fluency
bureaucracy	immediacy
candidacy	infancy
celibacy	intimacy
clemency	literacy
competency	lunacy
constancy	militancy
decency	privacy
delicacy	spicy
delinquency	urgency
democracy	vacancy
diplomacy	vagrancy

dom -- state, condition or quality of

boredom	kingdom
Christendom	martyrdom
dukedom	serfdom
earldom	stardom
freedom	wisdom

ee -- person or object recipient of this action

addressee	inductee
amputee	licensee
appointee	nominee
conferee	parolee
devotee	payee
divorcee	refugee
draftee	trainee
employee	transferee
escapee	trustee

eer -- one who is involved with

auctioneer	mutineer
balladeer	pistoleer
electioneer	profiteer
engineer	puppeteer
mountaineer	racketeer

en -- to cause, to have effect

blacken	moisten
brighten	sharpen
darken	strengthen
flatten	thicken
freshen	tighten
lengthen	toughen
lighten	weaken
loosen	widen

en -- resembling

drunken	olden
earthen	silken
golden	wooden
leaden	woolen
oaken	woven

ence -- quality or state of

absence	existence
affluence	indulgence
ambivalence	innocence
benevolence	magnificence
coherence	malevolence
competence	obedience
conference	patience
correspondence	penitence
deterrence	presence
difference	prevalence
excellence	violence

ency -- quality or state of

absorbency	excellency
deficiency	presidency
dependency	residency
equivalency	sufficiency

ent -- something which or someone who performs an action

dependent	opponent
descendent	resident
exponent	solvent
incumbent	student
nutrient	superintendent

ent -- behaving as, doing

absorbent	despondent
ambient	different
ambivalent	efficient
complacent	excellent
consistent	fluent

eous -- composed, having characteristics of

advantageous	gaseous
bounteous	homogeneous
courageous	instantaneous
curvaceous	plenteous
erroneous	righteous

ery -- art or practice of

archery	jobbery
bribery	robbery
cookery	snobbery
embroidery	sorcery
flattery	stitchery

er -- something that, someone who

achiever	dishwasher
angler	hitter
announcer	painter
archer	player
astronomer	runner
banker	singer
blotter	sitter
catcher	swimmer
cleaner	teacher
designer	teller

escense -- process, state of

acquiescence	luminescence
adolescence	obsolescence
convalescence	pubescence
effervescence	quiescence
iridescence	

ess -- one who does or is in a state of being (feminine)

actress	princess
empress	stewardess
heiress	waitress

ette -- small sized

cigarette	pipette
dinette	rosette
diskette	statuette
kitchenette	

form -- having the shape of

cuneiform	platform
free-form	waveform

ful -- quantity or number that fills

armful	mouthful
cupful	roomful
eyeful	spoonful
handful	

ful -- tending, causing

baneful	hopeful
beautiful	joyful
careful	painful
cheerful	peaceful
dreadful	plentiful
fearful	powerful
gainful	sorrowful
gleeful	tearful
hateful	watchful
helpful	wonderful

fy -- make, cause to be

beautify	modify
clarify	nullify
classify	pacify
dignify	qualify
diversify	rectify
emulsify	simplify
glorify	solidify
gratify	specify
horrify	terrify
justify	typify
liquefy	unify

graphic -- illustrated in writing

choreographic	telegraphic
geographic	topographic
oceanographic	typographic
pornographic	

hold -- grasp or possess

foothold	toehold
handhold	uphold
household	withhold
stronghold	

hood -- state, rank, condition

adulthood	likelihood
babyhood	manhood
bachelorhood	motherhood
boyhood	parenthood
brotherhood	priesthood
childhood	sisterhood
fatherhood	statehood
girlhood	widowhood
knighthood	womanhood

ia -- condition or state of

absentia	fantasia
amnesia	hysteria
anemia	insomnia
dyslexia	mania
euphoria	phobia

ial -- relating to

ceremonial	jovial
circumstantial	judicial
commercial	memorial
consequential	palatial
custodial	parochial
differential	pictorial
editorial	prejudicial
facial	presidential
familial	proverbial
financial	residential
glacial	secretarial
imperial	sequential
industrial	territorial
influential	trivial

ible -- being in the stage of or able to be

accessible	fallible
admissible	flexible
audible	horrible
collapsible	intelligible
combustible	permissible
comprehensible	reducible
convertible	reversible
corruptible	risible
credible	sensible
deductible	susceptible
defensible	tangible
digestible	transmissible
divisible	visible

ic -- having the form, nature or characteristic of

academic	democratic
acoustic	economic
alcoholic	heroic
alphabetic	idiotic
anesthetic	magnetic
aquatic	modernistic
autistic	optic
characteristic	romantic
civic	toxic

ical -- relating to

acoustical	pontifical
cylindrical	quizzical
ecological	rabbinical
geological	satirical
hypocritical	spherical
methodical	tactical
numerical	theatrical
periodical	theoretical
phonological	typographical
political	tyrannical

ician -- specialist, practitioner

academician	optician
diagnostician	pediatrician
electrician	physician
logician	politician
magician	rhetorician
mathematician	statistician
mortician	tactician
musician	technician
obstetrician	theoretician

ics -- relating to

academics	graphics
acrobatics	heroics
aerobics	hydraulics
athletics	linguistics
bymnastics	logistics
calisthenics	mathematics
dramatics	phonetics
dynamics	romantics
economics	statistics

ier -- person engaged in or connected with

amplifier	fortifier
cashier	furrier
cavalier	pacifier
clothier	warier
financier	worrier

ily -- in what manner

angrily	luckily
busily	merrily
cheerily	naughtily
cozily	readily
easily	sleepily
greedily	steadily
happily	temporarily
heavily	wearily
hungrily	worthily
lazily	

ious -- pertaining or relating to, resembling

ambitious	harmonious
devious	infectious
dubious	malicious
felonious	rebellious
glorious	suspicious

ish -- inclined to

babyish	girlish
bookish	pinkish
boyish	smallish
bullish	wolfish
foolish	youngish

ism -- action, condition

absenteeism	patriotism
alcoholism	pessimism
barbarism	pragmatism
cannibalism	racism
capitalism	realism
commercialism	sadism
cynicism	skepticism
hypnotism	symbolism
idealism	terrorism
magnetism	traditionalism
optimism	

ist -- doer, performer

artist
bicyclist
biologist
botanist
capitalist
columnist
dentist
hobbyist
humorist
hypnotist
lyricist
machinist
motorist
naturalist
pianist
realist
scientist
terrorist
therapist
tourist
typist
violinist
vocalist

istic -- referring to, characterized by

animalistic
antagonistic
atheistic
cannibalistic
characteristic
egotistic
expressionistic
humanistic
impressionistic
materialistic
monopolistic
naturalistic
optimistic
pessimistic
pluralistic
realistic
sadistic
simplistic
socialistic
theistic

itis -- inflammation of

appendicitis
arthritis
bronchitis
encephalitis
hepatitis
laryngitis
meningitis
neuritis
sinusitis
tonsillitis

ity -- quality or state of

acceptability
accountability
activity
brevity
capability
clarity
diversity
enormity
formality
frugality
levity
maturity
minority
mobility
necessity
profanity
profundity
radioactivity
reality
security
seniority
severity
suitability
tranquility
validity
vulgarity

ive -- tendency toward, disposition for

abusive
active
collective
competitive
constructive
creative
decorative
defective
defensive
digestive
effective
evasive
festive
impulsive
indicative
negative
preservative
relative
selective
talkative

ize -- act upon, make

alphabetize
capitalize
characterize
civilize
colonize
customize
economize
equalize
fertilize
finalize
maximize
optimize
realize
summarize
symbolize

less -- without

fearless
homeless
lifeless
odorless
penniless
powerless
priceless
purposeless
selfless
senseless
skinless
speechless
spotless
stainless
timeless
tireless
useless
weightless
wireless
worthless

let -- small

booklet
bracelet
circlet
cutlet
droplet
eyelet
ringlet
starlet

like -- like, alike

acidlike
businesslike
catlike
childlike
godlike
ladylike
lifelike
resinlike
statesmanlike
warlike

logy -- body of information

biology	mineralogy
climatology	physiology
criminology	radiology
entomology	sociology
geology	toxicology
genealogy	zoology

ly -- in what manner

actively	happily
adeptly	kindly
adequately	mechanically
affectionately	merrily
anxiously	naturally
badly	perfectly
boldly	precisely
calmly	properly
cautiously	quickly
distinctly	quietly
effectively	sweetly
gently	wisely

ly -- to what extent

barely	fundamentally
basically	hardly
broadly	largely
chiefly	merely
completely	narrowly
decidedly	primarily
endlessly	scarcely
fully	widely

lytic -- breaking down

analytic	hemolytic
catalytic	proteolytic
electrolytic	psychoanalytic

ma -- results of an action, state of

cinema	plasma
drama	prima
maxima	stigma
panorama	trauma

man (woman) -- person involved with

baseman	craftsman
boatman	fireman
businesswoman	fisherman
chairwoman	foreman
clergywoman	handyman
congresswoman	newspaperwoman
committeewoman	postman
councilwoman	sportswoman
countryman	statesman

manship -- art, characteristic

chairmanship	showmanship
craftsmanship	sportsmanship
horsemanship	statesmanship
marksmanship	workmanship
penmanship	

mate -- partner, associate

bunkmate	playmate
classmate	roommate
helpmate	shipmate
inmate	teammate

ment -- state of being

accompaniment	embellishment
achievement	employment
adornment	enchantment
advertisement	enforcement
amusement	enjoyment
argument	enlargement
assignment	enrollment
astonishment	investment
development	judgment
disarmament	movement

meter -- measure

accelerometer	odometer
altimeter	pedometer
barometer	pyrometer
calorimeter	speedometer
diameter	tachometer
hydrometer	thermometer
micrometer	

most -- to the superlative degree

foremost	outermost
hindmost	southernmost
innermost	topmost
leftmost	uppermost
northernmost	

ness -- state, condition, quality or degree

agelessness	coziness
aggressiveness	darkness
alertness	dizziness
appropriateness	dryness
baldness	effectiveness
bitterness	emptiness
brittleness	foolishness
calmness	goodness
candidness	happiness
carelessness	helplessness
cleanliness	illness
closeness	loneliness
clumsiness	readiness
consciousness	recklessness
coolness	silliness
coyness	soreness

oid -- shape, appearance of

alkaloid	planetoid
ameboid	rhomboid
asteroid	schizoid
ellipsoid	spheroid
lymphoid	tabloid
mongoloid	trapezoid
paranoid	

or -- something which or someone who performs an action

actor	debtor
advisor	director
assessor	editor
auditor	imitator
calculator	narrator
competitor	negotiator
conductor	predator
conspirator	regulator
councilor	sailor
creator	sensor

ory -- place used for an activity

armory	laboratory
conservatory	observatory
depository	preparatory
dormitory	repository
factory	

ory -- characterized by, relating to

ambulatory	excitatory
anticipatory	migratory
circulatory	obligatory
compensatory	predatory
discriminatory	regulatory

ous -- characteristic of

humorous	odorous
infectious	religious
joyous	tenuous
marvelous	various
mountainous	wondrous

proof -- safe from or protected against

childproof	shatterproof
fireproof	soundproof
foolproof	waterproof
rustproof	weatherproof

ship -- art or characteristic of

apprenticeship	fellowship
championship	friendship
citizenship	leadership
comradeship	membership
dealership	partnership
dictatorship	professorship

sion -- act, quality or state of

admission	extension
comprehension	fusion
compulsion	obsession
conclusion	omission
confession	permission
confusion	precision
decision	submission
depression	suspension
division	tension
emission	vision

sis -- action, process or result of

analysis
diagnosis
hydrolysis
hypnosis
mitosis

neurosis
paralysis
symbiosis
synthesis

some -- characterized by

awesome
bothersome
burdensome
lonesome
meddlesome

quarrelsome
tiresome
troublesome
venturesome
worrisome

some -- one of a group

foursome
threesome

twosome

ster -- person or thing associated with

gamester
gangster
mobster
oldster
pollster

prankster
roadster
songster
trickster
youngster

tion -- act, process or result of

abbreviation
acceleration
action
addition
collection
combination
complication
correction
decision
decoration
distortion
eruption
explanation
filtration
formation

graduation
gratification
indication
infection
information
injection
isolation
migration
nomination
operation
preservation
recommendation
reflection
repetition
sensation

tious -- pertaining, related to, resembling

ambitious
conscientious
contentious
expeditious
fictitious

ostentatious
pretentious
repetitious
superstitious
vexatious

tude -- quality, state of

amplitude
gratitude
ineptitude
latitude
longitude

magnitude
multitude
solicitude
solitude

ty -- quality, state of

arty
bratty
crafty
drifty
fatty
frosty
gusty
hearty

jaunty
knotty
loyalty
lusty
rusty
salty
velvety
witty

ular -- pertaining, relating to, resembling

angular
cellular
glandular
granular
molecular

popular
singular
triangular
tubular
vascular

ule -- small

globule
granule
lobule

nodule
ovule

ure -- quality or state of

closure
composure
curvature
departure
erasure
failure

fixture
forfeiture
legislature
moisture
procedure
seizure

ward -- in the direction of

afterward

downward

eastward

homeward

inward

leeward

northward

southward

upward

wayward

westward

windward

way -- path

airway

doorway

driveway

expressway

freeway

highway

railway

stairway

thruway

waterway

wise -- manner, means

clockwise

counterclockwise

crosswise

edgewise

leastwise

lengthwise

likewise

widthwise

work -- product or result of some type of labor or skill

artwork

basketwork

brickwork

bridgework

casework

clockwork

footwork

framework

guesswork

handiwork

homework

housework

legwork

patchwork

roadwork

schoolwork

steelwork

stonework

teamwork

woodwork

The Prefix, CO -- with, along or together with

Root words

author - one who writes a book or an article

operate - to work at something

exist - to be or to live

educational - pertaining to learning

habitat - a place where a person or animal usually lives

incident - something that happens or is happening

Derivatives (words made by adding the prefix, co)

coauthor - two or more authors write a book or article together

cooperate - to work together

coexist - to live along with

coeducational - an educational setting where boys and girls learn together

cohabit - two or more people or animals living in the same place

coincident - when two separate things occur at the same time

Read this passage and note how these derivatives are used. Answer the questions.

Mark Jones is a well-known history professor. He and his friend, Sam Reynolds are **co**authors of a book about the peaceful **co**existence of people in various countries. These experts have found that some people live in very crowded conditions and must **co**habit in very small homes. They found that the more willing the people were to **co**operate with each other, the happier they were.

Mark became so fond of some of the people whom he studied that he decided to leave his job as a professor for a year and work to build a school for the people in one of the small villages. It will be a simple building where both boys and girls will study. This **co**educational school will open in fall of next year, at the same time that Mark's book will be published. This is a nice **co**incidence.

1. What is Mark's book about?

2. What did Mark and Sam learn about the people who must live in crowded conditions?

3. Why will Mark leave his job as a professor for a year?

4. Who will attend the school which Mark will build? What kind of school will it be?

5. Could you buy a copy of Mark's book today? Why?

Review the root words. See how the prefix, **co** changes the meaning of each word.
These words are derivatives of the root words.

Select five derivatives from the list. Show how each was made below:

Prefix	*plus*	Root word	*equals*	Derivative
_____		_____		_____
_____		_____		_____
_____		_____		_____
_____		_____		_____
_____		_____		_____

Write a sentence with each of the derivatives using the prefix, **co.**

_____

_____

_____

_____

_____

Answer the questions following the passage.

_____

_____

_____

_____

_____

Just for fun, try writing your own story using as many of the derivatives as possible.

Root words

rail - parallel metal bars forming a track

activate - to make active or workable

toxic - poisonous

odorize - to add a scent or smell

compose - to put together

Derivatives (words made by adding the prefix, de)

derail - to come off of a track

deactivate - to cause to be inactive or not workable

detoxify - to remove a poisonous substance

deodorize - to remove a scent or smell

decompose - to take apart

Read this passage and note how these derivatives are used. Answer the questions.

The police rushed to the site of the **de**railed freight train. The train was carrying some dangerous materials, and everyone is afraid. There were some explosive devices on board which were **de**activated. Some poisonous materials spilled over hundreds of feet around the train. We are being told that experts would come in to **de**toxify this area. Some of the materials might cause a strong odor if they are exposed, so something will have to be done to **de**odorize the area. Some chemicals on board this train are so strong and dangerous that if they get near plants, the plants will die and **de**compose at once. I wish trains that carry such dangerous chemicals would not come so close to our town!

1. What kind of accident took place here?

2. What kinds of materials were on board the derailed train?

3. What might happen if some of the chemicals escape from the train cars?

4. How can we be sure that an accident like this won't happen near our town again?

Review the root words. See how the prefix, **de** changes the meaning of each word.
These words are derivatives of the root words. Show how each derivative was made.

Prefix	*plus*	**Root word**	*equals*	**Derivative**
_____		_____		_____
_____		_____		_____
_____		_____		_____
_____		_____		_____
_____		_____		_____

Write a sentence with each of the derivatives using the prefix, **de**.

_____

_____

_____

_____

_____

Answer the questions following the passage.

_____

_____

_____

_____

Just for fun, try writing your own story using as many of the derivatives as possible.

The Prefix, **dis** -- not or without

Root words

contented - satisfied

agree - to consent

respect - to show honor for

please - to be agreeable

obey - to carry out orders

connect - to join together

color - to give or add color

loyal - faithful to someone or one's country

like - to be pleased with

Derivatives (words made by adding the prefix, **dis**)

discontented - dissatisfied

disagree - to fail to consent

disrespect - to fail to show respect or honor

displease - to fail to please

disobey - to fail to carry out orders

disconnect - to break apart

discolor - to remove color

disloyal - not faithful

dislike - not to be pleased

Read this passage and note how these derivatives are used. Answer the questions.

> Mr. Hill has been **dis**contented lately with his son's **dis**agreeable attitude. Ken, his son, is usually a happy, good-natured boy, and this change in his behavior is puzzling. Sometimes Mr. Hill gives Ken chores to do, and Ken objects which causes arguments . Mr. Hill is angry over Ken's **dis**respect and is very **dis**pleased when Ken **dis**obeys. One day last week, Ken neglected to **dis**connect the hose when he was told to and water ran over the side of the wall. This caused some of the wood to **dis**color. Ken has also seemed to be **dis**loyal to his friends. Sometimes, he doesn't even talk to them when they call.
>
> Mr. and Mrs. Hill and Ken had a long talk. Ken said that one of his teachers appears to **dis**like him and often **dis**agrees with him in front of the class. He says that this has been upsetting him lately. Ken and his parents will meet with this teacher soon and try to straighten out the problem.

1. What seems different about Ken lately?

2. How does Mr. Hill feel about Ken's change in behavior?

3. Do we know of something that might be causing Ken to act differently these days?

4. What can be done about the problem?

Review the root words. See how the prefix, **dis** changes the meaning of each word.
These words are derivatives of the root words.

Select five derivatives from the list. Show how each was made below:

Prefix	*plus*	**Root word**	*equals*	**Derivative**
_____		_____		_____
_____		_____		_____
_____		_____		_____
_____		_____		_____
_____		_____		_____

Write a sentence with each of the derivatives using the prefix, **dis**.

_____

_____

_____

_____

_____

Answer the questions following the passage.

_____

_____

_____

_____

Just for fun, try writing your own story using as many of the derivatives as possible.

The Prefix, **en** -- to make; to put or place in the state of

Root words

danger - something that might cause injury or pain

code - a system of symbols for secret writing

circle - a round figure

able - capable of doing

trap - to catch

Derivatives (words made by adding the prefix, en)

endanger - to put into a dangerous situation

encode - to put into code, to make

encircle - to surround with a circle

enable - make able

entrap - to make someone or something ready to be trapped

Read this passage and note how these derivatives are used. Answer the questions.

We knew we were in trouble when the stranger came into the office and told us to get into the back room. We didn't wish to further **en**danger ourselves by screaming, so we went into the room as we were told. There, we **en**coded a message which we tapped with our feet and hoped that the people downstairs would hear.

They must have heard and understood us because soon afterward we heard voices out front, and we knew it was the police. Actually, the police had **en**circled the whole building to **en**able all the occupants to leave safely and to **en**trap the strangers .

1. Why did the people in the story think that they were in trouble?

2. How did they call for help?

3. How did the victims know that their call for help had been understood?

4. What did the police do to make sure everyone was safe and the burglars were caught?

Presentation Page: the Prefix, **en**

Review the root words. See how the prefix, **en** changes the meaning of each word. These words are derivatives of the root words. Show how each derivative was made.

Prefix	*plus*	Root word	*equals*	Derivative
_____		_____		_____
_____		_____		_____
_____		_____		_____
_____		_____		_____
_____		_____		_____

Write a sentence with each of the derivatives using the prefix, **en.**

_____

_____

_____

_____

_____

Answer the questions following the passage.

_____

_____

_____

Just for fun, try writing your own story using as many of the derivatives as possible.

Root words

possible - that which can be, exist, or happen

proper - suitable, appropriate, fitting

patient - calm tolerating delay or inconvenience; persevering

mature - developed; age appropriate

polite - courteous, using good manners

perfect - without faults or flaws

practical - useful, manageable

personal - private, individual

movable - able to be moved

Derivatives (words made by adding the prefix, im)

impossible - cannot be, exist or happen

improper - not suitable, appropriate, or fitting

impatient - unable to calmly tolerate delay or inconvenience

immature - not developed or age appropriate

impolite - discourteous, not using good manners

imperfect - flawed, having faults

impractical - difficult, not useful

impersonal - not private

immovable - impossible to be moved

Read this passage and note how these derivatives are used. Answer the questions.

> This morning the principal, Ms. Symms, told the students that it is **im**possible to tolerate some of the **im**proper behavior which she has observed in some students attending our school. She's becoming **im**patient with some of the **im**mature behavior and is most upset when students are **im**polite to one another.
>
> She said that she will punish such behavior by requiring students who act in such a way to come to school on Saturday and work. This might be an **im**perfect solution, and some families will find it **im**practical; but she feels that students must be taught that they are expected to behave properly and to respect each other. Ms. Symms is a very thoughtful and reasonable person. She will always listen to students and never treats people in an **im**personal manner. But she warned us not to try to change her mind about this because she is absolutely **im**movable.

1. Why is Ms. Symms upset?

2. What will she do about the problem?

3. Does she think that everyone will be pleased with her ideas about punishment?

4. Do you think that someone might be able to talk her out of her decision?

Review the root words. See how the prefix, **im** changes the meaning of each word. These words are derivatives of the root words.

Select five derivatives from the list. Show how each was made below:

Prefix	*plus*	**Root word**	*equals*	**Derivative**
_____		_____		_____
_____		_____		_____
_____		_____		_____
_____		_____		_____
_____		_____		_____

Write a sentence with each of the derivatives using the prefix, **im**.

_____

_____

_____

_____

_____

Answer the questions following the passage.

_____

_____

_____

_____

Just for fun, try writing your own story using as many of the derivatives as possible.

The Prefix, **in** -- not

Root words

visible - able to be seen

convenient - easy to do

dependent - relying on someone or something

audible - able to be heard

active - working; causing motion or change

direct - not interrupted, with nothing between

expensive - costly, having a high price

complete - finished

Derivatives (words made by adding the prefix, in)

invisible - not able to be seen

inconvenient - difficult to do

independent - depending on no one

inaudible - not able to be heard

inactive - not working or moving

indirect - interrupted

inexpensive - not very costly

incomplete - not finished

Read this passage and note how these derivatives are used. Answer the questions.

Our family is going to buy the newest household convenience available--the **in**visible robot! The robot will do many jobs around the house. It will wash dishes, do the laundry, clean the floors, and much more. It will also take care of jobs that can be quite **in**convenient like getting dinner ready and walking the dog. Having this robot will allow us to be more **in**dependent. Besides being **in**visible, it is completely **in**audible; and when it's **in**active, we don't even know where it is. No one will ever know we have a robot, even our guests! We can arrange for it to do jobs that we think of while we're not at home because it can be programmed **in**directly by way of any computer. Considering all the time that we'll save, it's a wonderful and **in**expensive household helper. So far, though, this **in**visible robot cannot be programmed to finish my **in**complete homework assignments.

1. What kinds of jobs can this amazing robot do?

2. Where do you think the writer's family will keep this new household convenience?

3. Why won't their friends know that they own this robot?

4. If you could have such a helper, what would you like to have it do for you?

Review the root words. See how the prefix, **in** changes the meaning of each word. These words are derivatives of the root words.

Select five derivatives from the list. Show how each was made below:

Prefix	*plus*	**Root word**	*equals*	**Derivative**
_____		_____		_____
_____		_____		_____
_____		_____		_____
_____		_____		_____
_____		_____		_____

Write a sentence with each of the derivatives using the prefix, **in**.

_____

_____

_____

_____

_____

Answer the questions following the passage.

_____

_____

_____

_____

Just for fun, try writing your own story using as many of the derivatives as possible.

The Prefixes, **in** -- inner, toward the inside and **out** -- outer, toward the outside

---

Root words

bound - headed in the direction of

board - being on a vehicle

put - to place, locate, thrust, or transfer something into a particular place

door - a structure for opening and closing a space which allows one to enter or leave a room or building

Derivatives (words made by adding the prefixes, **in** and **out**)

inbound - headed into a city or town

outbound - headed out of a city or town

inboard - being on the inside of a vehicle

outboard - being on the outside of a vehicle

input - what is put in as power to a machine, information into someone's mind, data into a computer

output - what is sent out as power from a machine, information from a person or data from a computer

indoor - within or on the inside of a building

outdoor - on the outside of a building

Read this passage and note how these derivatives are used. Answer the questions.

> When Harry rides the **in**bound morning train he looks for Luke, a real expert on motor boats. Harry would like to replace the **in**board motor on his small boat and hopes to find a motor which has better power **out**put. Even though Luke now has an **out**board motor on his boat, he's had boats with **in**board motors before. Harry is seeking information about boat motors from many different people. After he has enough **in**put, he will think about everything that he's learned and decide what kind of motor to buy.
>
> Harry and Luke enjoy talking about boating and water sports. They try to catch the same **in**bound and **out**bound trains as they travel into and out of the city each day. For the next several weeks, they'll be spending much time **in**doors because the weather is still too cold for **out**door fun; yet, they're both eager for springtime when they can enjoy their boats again!

1. What does Harry hope to learn by talking to Luke?

2. Do the men now have the same kinds of motorboats?

3. How will Harry decide what kind of motor to buy for his boat?

4. Do you think that Harry and Luke might make plans to go boating this weekend?

Review the root words. See how the prefixes, **in** and **out** change the meaning of each word. These words are derivatives of the root words.

Select five derivatives from the list. Show how each was made below:

Prefix	*plus*	**Root word**	*equals*	**Derivative**
_____		_____		_____
_____		_____		_____
_____		_____		_____
_____		_____		_____
_____		_____		_____

Write a sentence with each of the derivatives using the prefixes, **in** or **out**.

_____

_____

_____

_____

_____

Answer the questions following the passage.

_____

_____

_____

_____

Just for fun, try writing your own story using as many of the derivatives as possible.

The Prefixes, **inter** -- among or between, and **intra** -- within

Root words

mural - wall

school - a place for learning

state - a group of people organized under one government

faith - what one believes

personal - individual, private

nation - a stable community of people with a territory, history, culture, and language in common

planet - a heavenly body that revolves around the sun

Derivatives (words made by adding the prefixes, **inter** and **intra**)

intramural - within the walls

interschool - between or among schools

intraschool - within a school

interstate - between or among states

intrastate - within a state

interfaith - between or among people of different beliefs

interpersonal - between persons

international - between or among nations

interplanetary - between or among planets

Read this passage and note how these derivatives are used. Answer the questions.

> Ms. Wright has always been very good at organizing events. When she was principal at our school she organized a wonderful **intra**mural music contest. The following year, other schools heard of the contest, and it soon became an **inter**school event in our town. She was also responsible for starting the first **intra**state high school art exhibit. High school students from all over our state display their work at this exhibit every spring.
>
> Now, Ms. Wright is moving to something extraordinary. She's organizing an **inter**faith, **inter**state meeting where people from many different backgrounds will get together to discuss all types of issues, from **inter**personal relations to **inter**national affairs. She hopes that this gathering will help people to understand each other better and work for peace. If this meeting is successful, Ms. Wright hopes that it will become an annual **inter**state, **inter**national, or, someday even, an annual **inter**planetary event!

1. What did Ms. Wright organize while she was a principal?

2. What kinds of cultural events got started because of this woman?

3. Is she still the school principal?

4. What is she working on now?

5. What will happen if she has success this year?

Review the root words. See how the prefixes, **inter** and **intra** change the meaning of each word. These words are derivatives of the root words.

Select five derivatives from the list. Show how each was made below:

Prefix	*plus*	**Root word**	*equals*	**Derivative**
_____		_____		_____
_____		_____		_____
_____		_____		_____
_____		_____		_____
_____		_____		_____

Write a sentence with each of the derivatives using the prefixes, **inter** or **intra**.

_____

_____

_____

_____

_____

Answer the questions following the passage.

_____

_____

_____

_____

_____

Just for fun, try writing your own story using as many of the derivatives as possible.

The Prefix, **mal** -- bad or improper

Root words	Derivatives (words made by adding the prefix, **mal**)
formed - shaped or developed according to an expected pattern	**malformed** - not formed properly
nutrition - nourishment or intake and digestion of food needed by the body	**malnutrition** - not properly nourished
occlusion - closing properly	**malocclusion** - when things do not line up to close properly
function - the natural characteristic action or purpose of something or someone	**malfunction** - not functioning properly
adjusted - settled or situated correctly in one's surroundings	**maladjusted** - not settled or situated correctly
practice - to work at as a profession	**malpractice** - improper professional work or conduct

Read this passage and note how these derivatives are used. Answer the questions.

> I don't think Jan would make a very good scientist. She tried to build a robot to help her with her homework. She put together all the parts, but the robot is terribly **mal**formed. The eyes and ears are in the wrong places, and the sensory channels are miswired. The nose is crooked and not connected to the control box. The teeth do not line up and close properly.
>
> This poor robot will have a hard time trying to see or hear, and it can't smell at all. Robots don't need to chew up food because they don't need to eat, and that's good. This one would surely be **mal**nourished with that dental **mal**occlusion!
>
> Looks like Jan will be doing her homework by herself. This robot will surely **mal**function. If this unfortunate, **mal**adjusted creature would come to life, he'd probably sue Jan for scientific **mal**practice!

1.   Why did Jan build a robot?

2.   Why couldn't the robot see, hear, or smell?

3.   What would happen if the robot would have to eat in order to survive?

4.   Will Jan's homework become easier because of this robot?

Review the root words. See how the prefix, **mal** changes the meaning of each word.
These words are derivatives of the root words.

Select five derivatives from the list. Show how each was made below:

Prefix	*plus*	**Root word**	*equals*	**Derivative**
_____		_____		_____
_____		_____		_____
_____		_____		_____
_____		_____		_____
_____		_____		_____

Write a sentence with each of the derivatives using the prefix, **mal**.

_____

_____

_____

_____

_____

Answer the questions following the passage.

_____

_____

_____

_____

Just for fun, try writing your own story using as many of the derivatives as possible.

The Prefix, **mis** -- wrong, done incorrectly

Root words

pronounce - to say clearly

understand - to know the meaning of what is spoken or written

spell - to write or name the letters in a word

print - to make a mark on a surface

inform - to give information

handle - to manipulate with one's hands

place - to put into a particular place

behave - to act properly

Derivatives (words made by adding the prefix, **mis**)

mispronounce - to say something in a way that is not clear

misunderstand - to fail to know the meaning of something

misspell - to incorrectly arrange the letters of a word

misprint - to make an incorrect mark

misinform - to give someone incorrect information

mishandle - to handle something improperly

misplace - to put something in the wrong place

misbehave - to act improperly

Read this passage and note how these derivatives are used. Answer the questions.

> We planned to give Mom a recording of her favorite symphony for her birthday, but the record didn't arrive on time. We're not sure why. Perhaps we **mis**pronounced our name or the name of the symphony composer when we ordered the record. Or, possibly the clerk **mis**understood us. Possibly the clerk **mis**spelled or **mis**printed the information when she sent the order to the warehouse. Possibly, we were **mis**informed as to how long it should take for the record to arrive. Also, it's possible that the record was **mis**handled and damaged in shipment. Maybe it really was delivered to our record shop but was somehow **mis**placed. But, I'm sure that Mom will forgive us for being late with her birthday present, just like she always forgave us for **mis**behaving!

1. Why couldn't the children give their mother the record for her birthday as they had planned?

2. What might the children have done incorrectly as they ordered the record?

3. What could the clerk at the record store have done incorrectly?

4. Did the children decide to give their mom a different gift so that she would have a present from them on her birthday?

Review the root words. See how the prefix, **mis** changes the meaning of each word. These words are derivatives of the root words.

Select five derivatives from the list. Show how each was made below:

Prefix	*plus*	**Root word**	*equals*	**Derivative**
_____		_____		_____
_____		_____		_____
_____		_____		_____
_____		_____		_____
_____		_____		_____

Write a sentence with each of the derivatives using the prefix, **mis**.

_____

_____

_____

_____

_____

Answer the questions following the passage.

_____

_____

_____

_____

Just for fun, try writing your own story using as many of the derivatives as possible.

The Prefixes, **pre** -- before and **post** -- after

Root words

view - to see

season - the time when something takes place

arrange - to organize

cook - to prepare food by boiling, baking, frying or steaming

bake - to cook by dry heat in an oven

school - a place for learning

graduate - one who has completed a course of study

war - armed conflict between nations

historic - based on people or recorded events of the past

game - a sport involving competition under rules

Derivatives (words made by adding the prefixes, **pre** and **post**)

preview - to see something before its scheduled time

preseason - before the season

postseason - occurring after a particular season

prearrange - to organize ahead of time

precooked - cooked at an earlier time

prebaked - baked at an earlier time

preschool - a learning setting for children between infancy and school age

postgraduate - occurring after one completes a course of study

prewar - before a war

postwar - occurring after a war

prehistoric - something which occurred before history was written

pregame - occurring before a game

Read this passage and note how these derivatives are used. Answer the questions.

We had a chance to **pre**view the our city's football team in a **pre**season game last weekend. Before the game, we went to a **pre**arranged tailgate picnic. The food was delicious. Someone brought some **pre**cooked chili and some **pre**baked rolls. Others brought salads and desserts.

It was so much fun! The day was most interesting because there were so many people with different jobs and backgrounds. There was a **pre**school teacher who taught some of the football players' children, and she got to talk to the players every day. Also, I met a **post**graduate student who was studying the difference between **pre**war and **post**war culture in Europe. She'd been to Europe and the Soviet Union several times. Last year, she saw the Bolshoi Ballet perform. Her husband is an anthropologist who is an expert in **pre**historic animals. There were several other interesting people there as well.

We had so much fun that we made plans to get together for some other **pre**game picnics during football season and have a **post**season party some time after the holidays.

1. What time of year did this party and game take place?
2. What kinds of food were brought to the party?
3. Why do you suppose that this kind of party might be called a "tailgate" party?
4. How can we be quite sure that the people enjoyed themselves on this day?

Review the root words. See how the prefixes, **pre** and **post** change the meaning of each word. These words are derivatives of the root words.

Select five derivatives from the list. Show how each was made below:

Prefix	*plus*	**Root word**	*equals*	**Derivative**
_____		_____		_____
_____		_____		_____
_____		_____		_____
_____		_____		_____
_____		_____		_____

Write a sentence with each of the derivatives using the prefixes, **pre** or **post**.

_____

_____

_____

_____

_____

Answer the questions following the passage.

_____

_____

_____

_____

Just for fun, try writing your own story using as many of the derivatives as possible.

Root words

decorate - to paint and wallpaper

furnish - to supply with furniture

write - to form letters on a surface with a pen

state - to express

read - to understand by interpreting printed letters

copy - to make something just like another

tell - to express by speaking

discover - to learn of the existence of

Derivatives (words made by adding the prefix, **re**)

redecorate - to decorate in a new way

refurnish - to furnish again

rewrite - to write something again

restate - to say something again

reread - to read something again

recopy - to copy something again

retell - to tell something again

rediscover - to discover something again

Read this passage and note how these derivatives are used. Answer the questions.

Bill was so excited that his parents were planning to **re**decorate and **re**furnish his room that he decided to write his English paper about this project.

Unfortunately, he spent so much time selecting new furniture and paint that he didn't have time to do a good job on the English paper. He handed in a sloppy paper with many mistakes.

His teacher made him **re**write the paper. He **re**stated many items and **re**defined some of the words. This time he **re**read it many times to check for mistakes. He copied the paper over to make sure it was neat, then **re**copied it just to make extra sure.

Bill tells the story of his messy paper whenever he sees someone doing something fast and in a sloppy way. He **re**discovered how important it is to concentrate on working carefully.

1. How did Bill choose the topic for his English paper?

2. Was his teacher satisfied with the paper the first time he handed it in?

3. What did Bill do differently when he prepared the paper the second time?

4. What does Bill tell his friends about neatness?

Review the root words. See how the prefix, **re** changes the meaning of each word. These words are derivatives of the root words.

Select five derivatives from the list. Show how each was made below:

Prefix	*plus*	**Root word**	*equals*	**Derivative**
_____		_____		_____
_____		_____		_____
_____		_____		_____
_____		_____		_____
_____		_____		_____

Write a sentence with each of the derivatives using the prefix, **re**.

_____

_____

_____

_____

_____

Answer the questions following the passage.

_____

_____

_____

_____

Just for fun, try writing your own story using as many of the derivatives as possible.

Root words

annual - yearly

formal - according to fixed customs, rules, style of dress

final - the last in a series of events

circle - a round figure

precious - very costly or valuable.

sweet - not bitter, sugar-tasting

Derivatives (words made by adding the prefix, **semi**)

semiannual - twice each year

semiformal - style of dress or costume partially, but not fully formal

semifinal - next to the last in a series of events

semicircle -half of a round figure

semiprecious - referring to gems of lower value than precious gems

semisweet - not bitter, but not sweet

Read this passage and note how these derivatives are used. Answer the questions.

> Katie's high school arranges two dress-up dances each year. These dances are held **semi**annually, one in October and one in April. The style of dress is not casual but not quite formal. Actually, it's a **semi**formal dance.
>
> This year awards will be given to the best dancers in the school. Katie and her partner, Josh, have a good chance to win. They have made it all the way to the **semi**finals, which will be held the day before the dance.
>
> Katie wants to look nice. Her mom is making her a dress out of a fabric designed with various shapes, squares, triangles, circles, and **semi**circles. The dress will look nice with the bracelet of silver and **semi**precious stones which Katie bought last year in Arizona.
>
> As a "thank-you" gift, Katie bought her mom a box of **semi**sweet chocolates, her mom's favorite kind of candy.

1. Why is the dance considered a semiformal?

2. Why does she think that she and Josh have a chance to win the dance contest?

3. What will she wear to the dance?

4. How did Kate show that she appreciated her mom making the dress?

Review the root words. See how the prefix, **semi** changes the meaning of each word. These words are derivatives of the root words.

Select five derivatives from the list. Show how each was made below:

Prefix	*plus*	**Root word**	*equals*	**Derivative**
_____		_____		_____
_____		_____		_____
_____		_____		_____
_____		_____		_____
_____		_____		_____

Write a sentence with each of the derivatives using the prefix, **semi.**

_____

_____

_____

_____

_____

Answer the questions following the passage.

_____

_____

_____

_____

Just for fun, try writing your own story using as many of the derivatives as possible.

The Prefix, **sub** -- below or beneath, a smaller amount, less important

Root words

urban - that which is in a city

marine - refers to sea or water

compact - something designed so that the parts fit close together to take up less space

committee - a group of people who study or support something together

contractor - someone who signs a contract agreeing to do something

floor - the bottom surface

zero - the lowest point

Derivatives (words made by adding the prefix, **sub**)

suburban - an area smaller than and outside of a city

submarine - a ship which is operated below the water

subcompact - smaller than a standard compact item

subcommittee - a division of a committee

subcontractor - a contractor hired by another contractor

subfloor - a rough floor below the finished floor

subzero - below the lowest point

Read this passage and note how these derivatives are used. Answer the questions.

Jack, who lives in a **sub**urb of Boise was stationed on a **sub**marine in the Navy for four years. Now he's a busy and active citizen in his community. In addition to his job selling **sub**compact cars, he serves on a government **sub**committee concerned with the preservation of wildlife. He's supervising the construction of a new shelter for outdoor education in a national forest in Idaho. Just last week a **sub**contractor completed the foundation, frame, and **sub**floor of the shelter. Jack must make sure that the shelter can withstand heavy snow and **sub**zero temperatures which often occur in the area.

All of us who live in this community feel fortunate to have a neighbor like Jack. We enjoy his **sub**marine stories and are pleased that he works so hard to help us understand so much about nature and animals.

1. What did Jack do while he was in the Navy?

2. What does Jack do for a living now?

3. What is Jack interested in besides selling cars?

4. What will the structure that Jack is helping to build be used for?

5. How do Jack's neighbors feel about him?

Review the root words. See how the prefix, **sub** changes the meaning of each word. These words are derivatives of the root words.

Select five derivatives from the list. Show how each was made below:

Prefix	plus	Root word	equals	Derivative
_____		_____		_____
_____		_____		_____
_____		_____		_____
_____		_____		_____
_____		_____		_____

Write a sentence with each of the derivatives using the prefix, **sub.**

_____

_____

_____

_____

_____

Answer the questions following the passage.

_____

_____

_____

_____

_____

Just for fun, try writing your own story using as many of the derivatives as possible.

The Prefix, **super** -- above, over, beyond

Root words

star - an outstanding performer

human -having the characteristics of mankind

sensitive - keenly aware of surroundings and feelings

natural - of or dealing with nature

ordinary - customary, usual, common

power - strength or influence

modern - the style of today

huge - very large

sonic- a term referring to the sound which people can hear

Derivatives (words made by adding the prefix, **super**)

superstar - a performer who is outstanding even beyond other star performers

superhuman - having characteristics beyond those of humans

supersensitive - very keenly aware of surroundings and feelings, beyond the ordinary

supernatural - beyond that which is natural

superordinary - above and beyond what is ordinary

superpower - a nation of outstanding world power

supermodern - the most modern design possible today

superhuge - very, very large

supersonic - beyond the speed at which sound travels

Read this passage and note how these derivatives are used. Answer the questions.

> MacDuff is a real **super**star. His **super**human strength and **super**sensitive perception make us think he must be **super**natural. Besides extraordinary strength and understanding, he's an outstanding musician and a superior speaker. We don't hear of him too often because he choses to share his **super**ordinary talents and skills with the people from underdeveloped countries. Although **super**power nations try endlessly to convince him to perform in their **super**modern arenas for **super**huge audiences, he prefers to perform for small groups of people who live in places where well-known performers don't usually travel. In fact, he travels as fast as he can in a **super**sonic aircraft, if possible, so he can reach many small underdeveloped countries. He receives no money for his work, only applause and smiles from thousands of people each year. MacDuff certainly is a **super**star.

1.   What makes MacDuff a superstar?

2.   Where does he like to perform?

3.   How does he travel?

4.   Do you think that MacDuff is a wealthy person?

5.   What is meant by an underdeveloped country?

Review the root words. See how the prefix, **super** changes the meaning of each word.
These words are derivatives of the root words.

Select five derivatives from the list. Show how each was made below:

Prefix	*plus*	Root word	*equals*	Derivative
_____		_____		_____
_____		_____		_____
_____		_____		_____
_____		_____		_____
_____		_____		_____

Write a sentence with each of the derivatives using the prefix, **super**.

_____

_____

_____

_____

_____

Answer the questions following the passage.

_____

_____

_____

_____

Just for fun, try writing your own story using as many of the derivatives as possible.

The Prefix, **tele** -- far

Root words

scope - an instrument for observing

vision - sight, something that we see

photo - a word part meaning produced by light as a camera is used to produce pictures

gram - a word part referring to something written

phone - a word part referring to an instrument for producing or transmitting sound

Derivatives (words made by adding the prefix, **tele**)

telescope - an instrument for enlarging a distant image

television - an instrument which enables one to see something which is happening far away

telephoto - a camera lens which produces a large image of a distant object using film, a light-sensitive surface

telegram - a coded message sent over a distance electronically

telephone - an instrument used for transmitting sound over a distance

Read this passage and note how these derivatives are used. Answer the questions.

> Wendy has made some amazing discoveries while looking through her **tele**scope. She has become very famous for her work. Last week, she appeared on **tele**vision. She had tried to take some pictures with her **tele**photo lens hoping to show them on the program, but they did not turn out. She did, however, present some very interesting information. After the program she received many letters and **tele**grams. She even got a **tele**phone call from the president.

1. Where, most likely, are the things which Wendy had discovered?

2. Did Wendy do what she had planned to do when she appeared on television?

3. Was her television appearance important? Why do you think so?

Review the root words. See how the prefix, **tele** changes the meaning of each word. These words are derivatives of the root words. Show how each derivative was made.

Prefix	*plus*	**Root word**	*equals*	**Derivative**
_____		_____		_____
_____		_____		_____
_____		_____		_____
_____		_____		_____
_____		_____		_____

Write a sentence with each of the derivatives using the prefix, **tele**.

_____

_____

_____

_____

_____

Answer the questions following the passage.

_____

_____

_____

Just for fun, try writing your own story using as many of the derivatives as possible.

The Prefix, **trans** -- across, over, through

Root words

plant - to put something into the ground to grow

port - a word part meaning to carry

Atlantic - the ocean which touches North and South America to the west and Europe and Africa to the east.

Pacific - the largest ocean; the ocean extending between Asia and North and South America

oceanic - pertaining to an ocean, a large body of salt water

continental - referring to any of the large main land areas of the earth

Derivatives (words made by adding the prefix, trans)

transplant - to move an entire plant from where it was planted over to another area and plant it here

transport - to carry something over a distance

transatlantic - crossing over the Atlantic Ocean

transpacific - crossing over the Pacific Ocean

transoceanic - crossing over an ocean

transcontinental - crossing over a continent

Read this passage and note how these derivatives are used. Answer the questions.

> Our science teacher told us about a very unusual plant that grows in the African jungle. It can be **trans**planted and should grow in most warm areas. It produces a very nourishing fruit.
>
> Some farmers plan to bring some of these plants to this country this spring and try to grow this wonderful fruit here. They will **trans**port these plants on special planes. There will be several **trans**atlantic and **trans**pacific flights, since they plan to bring theses plants to many different parts of this country. These **trans**oceanic and **trans**continental flights must be on time, and the farmers must have many workers ready and waiting to work. This plant must be **trans**planted within 48 hours from the time that it was removed from the African soil.

1. Where does this unusual plant grow?

2. Do we have any of these plants growing in our country now?

3. How do the farmers in our country plan to get this plant to grow in our country?

4. Why do farmers want to raise these plants?

5. Why do the farmers have to move so quickly?

Review the root words. See how the prefix, **trans** changes the meaning of each word.
These words are derivatives of the root words.

Select five derivatives from the list. Show how each was made below:

Prefix	*plus*	**Root word**	*equals*	**Derivative**
_____		_____		_____
_____		_____		_____
_____		_____		_____
_____		_____		_____
_____		_____		_____

Write a sentence with each of the derivatives using the prefix, **trans**.

_____

_____

_____

_____

_____

Answer the questions following the passage.

_____

_____

_____

_____

Just for fun, try writing your own story using as many of the derivatives as possible.

The Prefix, **up** -- in a higher direction and **down** -- in a lower direction

Root words

swing - swaying from one direction to another

stairs - a series of steps between levels

hill - a raised part of the earth

stream - a small river whose current moves in a particular direction

grade - a step or level in one direction

turn - to change course

Derivatives (words made by adding the prefixes, **up** and **down**)

upswing - swaying in an upward direction

downswing - swinging in a downward direction

upstairs - on an upper floor

uphill - toward the top of a hill

downhill - moving toward the bottom of a hill

upstream - in the direction opposite to the current of a stream

upgrade - to raise in value or quantity

downgrade - move to a lower value or quantity

upturn - to change course moving in an upward direction

Read this passage and note how these derivatives are used. Answer the questions.

Bruce noticed an **up**swing in his grades after his study hall was moved to the **up**stairs library. Before, the students studied **down**stairs near the cafeteria where there was much noise, poor lighting, and no dictionaries or encyclopedias. Concentrating in these conditions was an **up**hill battle; Bruce felt as though he was swimming **up**stream against a strong current! He is grateful that the principal **up**graded the study conditions at school. He thinks that the **up**turn in his grades will continue. He knows that a **down**swing in grades will be no one's fault but his own. He cannot blame **down**graded study conditions!

1. Are Bruce's grades getting better or worse?

2. Why is it easier to study in the upstairs library than downstairs near the cafeteria?

3. Do we know of any reason why Bruce's grades might go down?

Review the root words. See how the prefixes, **up** and **down** changes the meaning of each word. These words are derivatives of the root words.

Select five derivatives from the list. Show how each was made below:

Prefix	*plus*	Root word	*equals*	Derivative
_____		_____		_____
_____		_____		_____
_____		_____		_____
_____		_____		_____
_____		_____		_____

Write a sentence with each of the derivatives using the prefix, **up** or **down**.

_____

_____

_____

_____

_____

Answer the questions following the passage.

_____

_____

_____

Just for fun, try writing your own story using as many of the derivatives as possible.

The Prefixes, **uni** -- one, **bi** -- two and **tri** -- three

Root words

cycle - round, wheel

angle - the shape formed when two plane surfaces meet

plane - a vehicle kept up by the force of air on its wings

focal - refers to being in focus

ped - a word part meaning foot

centennial - a celebration of something which has lasted for a hundred years

Derivatives (words made by adding the prefixes, **uni**, **bi** and **tri**)

unicycle - a vehicle having only one wheel

bicycle - a vehicle having two wheels

tricycle - a vehicle having three wheels

triangle - a shape with three sides and three angles

biplane - an airplane with two sets of wings, one above the other

bifocal - a pair of glasses where one part of the lens is for close focus and another part is for distant focus

tripod - a three-legged device for setting up a camera

bicentennial - a two-hundred-year celebration

triplets - three children born at a single birth

Read this passage and note how these derivatives are used. Answer the questions.

> We live in the best neighborhood in Cincinnati. There are many nice families in our neighborhood. On one side of our house, there's a family with three-year-old twins. On the other side, lives a family with **tri**plets. The **tri**plets are the same age as me, nine years old. We play ball and ride **bi**cycles together. We take turns riding my **uni**cycle. The twins like to ride their **tri**cycles. Also, they like to play in their **tri**angle-shaped sandbox which their grandpa made last year when he flew into Cincinnati in his **bi**plane.
>
> Last Saturday after my dad picked up his new **bi**focals, he set his camera on the **tri**pod and took some pictures of all of us. He said he wants lots of pictures so we can remember the things that we did this year. It's a very special year for us. This year Cincinnati celebrates its **bi**centennial.

1. Is the writer satisfied with where he or she lives? How do you know?

2. What do the twins do when they play?

3. Where do the twins play that is unusual?

4. Why is this a special year in Cincinnati?

Review the root words. See how the prefixes, **uni, bi,** and **tri** change the meaning of each word. These words are derivatives of the root words.

Select five derivatives from the list. Show how each was made below:

Prefix	*plus*	**Root word**	*equals*	**Derivative**
_____		_____		_____
_____		_____		_____
_____		_____		_____
_____		_____		_____
_____		_____		_____

Write a sentence with each of the derivatives using the prefix, **uni, bi,** or **tri.**

_____

_____

_____

_____

_____

Answer the questions following the passage.

_____

_____

_____

_____

The Suffix, **able** -- tending to or fit for

Root words

port - a word part meaning to carry

remove - to move something from where it is

notice - to pay attention to

fashion - current style

wash - to clean with water or other liquid

suit - appropriate to

enjoy - to get joy or pleasure from

use - to put into action or service

exchange - to trade

return - to bring or send back

refund - to give back

Derivatives (words made by adding the suffix, **able**)

portable - fit for carrying

removable - fit for being moved

noticeable - tending to pay attention

fashionable - tending to be in style currently

washable - fit for cleaning with water

suitable - tending to be appropriate

enjoyable - fit for getting pleasure from

usable - fit for being put into use or service

exchangeable - fit for being traded

returnable - fit for bringing or sending back

refundable - fit for giving back

Read this passage and note how these derivatives are used. Answer the questions.

> Carol was pleased to find the perfect wedding gift for her niece, Susan. She found a port**able**, lightweight picnic table. The table folds up and has remov**able** legs. When it's not being used, it is hardly notic**eable** and can be stored almost anywhere. Along with the picnic table, Carol will give her niece a set of fashion**able** napkins and placemats which are wash**able** and easy to take care of. Carol is sure that the table, placemats, and napkins are suit**able** gifts for Susan and her new husband. She hopes that they will have many enjoy**able** dinners using them. If Susan and her husband do not feel that these things are us**able** she can take them back to the store. Carol made sure that the picnic table as well as the placemat and napkin set were exchang**eable** or return**able** and that the money was refund**able**.

1. Can the picnic table be moved easily from one place to another? Why?

2. When the table is not in use do you think it would be noticeable?

3. Which parts of the table can be taken off?

4. Why might Susan and her new husband take the picnic table and linen set back to the store?

5. If they decided to return these gifts would they get money back? Why?

Review the root words. See how the suffix, **able** changes the meaning of each word. These words are derivatives of the root words.

Select five derivatives from the list. Show how each was made below:

Root word	*plus*	Suffix	*equals*	Derivative
_____		_____		_____
_____		_____		_____
_____		_____		_____
_____		_____		_____
_____		_____		_____

Write a sentence with each of the derivatives using the suffix, **able**.

_____

_____

_____

_____

_____

Answer the questions following the passage.

_____

_____

_____

_____

_____

Just for fun, try writing your own story using as many of the derivatives as possible.

The Suffix, **age** -- an amount, collection or number of something; the condition, stage, function or result of something

Root words

wreck - remains of something that's been destroyed

lug- to carry with effort

leak - to accidentally let a fluid out

mile - a measure of distance

dose - an amount of medicine to be taken at one time

percent - rate

link - anything that connects

patron - a regular customer

Derivatives (words made by adding the suffix, **age**)

wreckage - collection of remains of destroyed materials

luggage - a collection of bags to be filled and carried

leakage - an amount of fluid which is accidentally let out

mileage - an amount of miles

dosage - the number of doses of medicine to be taken during a period of time

percentage - a particular amount or part of a whole

linkage - the condition of being linked

patronage - the state of being a regular customer.

Read this passage and note how the derivatives are used. Answer the questions.

The wreck**age** and destruction at the accident scene amazed even the experienced law officers on duty. Tools and lugg**age** were scattered for hundreds of feet. The car's fuel and oil lines were smashed and broken, and the carpeting and upholstery had soaked up the leak**age**. The car was badly damaged, and probably could not be repaired. It had been a beautiful car having many luxuries. It had a sporty design was comfortable to drive and had gotten good gas mile**age**.

The driver was badly hurt and had been taken to the hospital. She was given a small dose of medicine to fight infections, but the doctors increased the dos**age** because she had so many cuts and bruises. She and her friends had been drinking at a bar just outside of town. Many college students go to this bar on weekends. A large percent**age** of these students live north of town, just up this road. The police claim a link**age** between the students'patron**age** at this bar and the number of accidents that occur on this road.

1.   What did the police officers see at the accident scene?

2.   In what condition were the upholstery and carpets? What was the reason for this.

3.   What do you know about the amount of gasoline that this car had used?

4.   Why do the police think that there are so many accidents on this road?

Review the root words. See how the suffix, **age** changes the meaning of each word. These words are derivatives of the root words.

Select five derivatives from the list. Show how each was made below:

Root word	*plus*	Suffix	*equals*	Derivative
_____		_____		_____
_____		_____		_____
_____		_____		_____
_____		_____		_____
_____		_____		_____

Write a sentence with each of the derivatives using the suffix, **age**.

_____

_____

_____

_____

_____

Answer the questions following the passage.

_____

_____

_____

_____

Just for fun, try writing your own story using as many of the derivatives as possible.

Root words

occupy - to take up space

serve - to work for someone

account - to keep financial matters in order

apply - to make a request

inform - to give information

tyr - a word part referring to harshness or cruelty

merc - a word part referring to wares or merchandise

Derivatives (words made by adding the suffix, **ant**)

occupant - one who takes up space

servant - someone who works for someone else

accountant - one who keeps financial matters in order

applicant - one who makes a request

informant - one who gives information

tyrant - one who is harsh and cruel to others

merchant - one who deals with wares or merchandise

Read this passage and note how the derivatives are used. Answer the questions.

Rumor has it that the occup**ant** of the house on Pinacle Hill was a millionaire. He had no family but some serv**ant**s lived in the house with him. Bankers, account**ant**s, and lawyers sometimes came to the house, probably on business. He was a mysterious man. No one knew much about him. Those who had worked for him sent applications to a lawyer's office, and the applic**ant**s were interviewed by the lawyer. All that went on in the house was a secret, but once an inform**ant** told a local merch**ant** that this man was a ty**rant** and that his employees were afraid of him.

1. Who lived in the house on Pinacle Hill? What do you know about him?

2. Did anyone ever come to the house?

3. If someone wanted to work for the person who lived in the house on Pinacle Hill, what would he or she have to do in order to get a job?

4. How do you think anyone found out anything about this mysterious man? Did the believe what they heard?

5. Would you enjoy working for this man?

Review the root words. See how the suffix, **ant** changes the meaning of each word. These words are derivatives of the root words.

Select five derivatives from the list. Show how each was made below:

Root word	*plus*	**Suffix**	*equals*	**Derivative**
_____		_____		_____
_____		_____		_____
_____		_____		_____
_____		_____		_____
_____		_____		_____

Write a sentence with each of the derivatives using the suffix, **ant**.

_____

_____

_____

_____

_____

Answer the questions following the passage.

_____

_____

_____

_____

_____

Just for fun, try writing your own story using as many of the derivatives as possible.

The Suffix, **dom** -- the state, condition or quality of

Root words

king - a male ruler of a state

wise - having good judgement and knowledge

duke - the highest ranking nobleman below a prince

earl - a nobleman

serf - a servant

bored - uninterested

free - able to do as one chooses

star - an outstanding performer

Derivatives (words made by adding the suffix, **dom**)

kingdom - a territory which is under the rule of a king

wisdom - the quality of showing knowledge and judgement

dukedom - the state of being a duke

earldom - the state of being an earl

serfdom - the state of being a servant

boredom - the condition of being uninterested

freedom - conditions under which one can make choices

stardom - being an outstanding performer

Read this passage and note how the derivatives are used. Answer the questions.

The king**dom** of Whimsyville is a wonderful place to live. King Whimsy enjoys working and playing right along with the town people, yet he has the wis**dom** to rule. In Whimsyville, all people are equal. No one ever thinks of knighthood, duke**dom**, or earl**dom**. Nor does anyone have to fear serf**dom**. Everyone is busy and productive; there's no bore**dom** in Whimsyville. People enjoy the free**dom** to work according to their own ideas. They might reach any goal which they work toward: knowledge, wealth, strength, friendship, even star**dom**.

1. Is King Whimsy a tyrant? How do you know?

2. Are the people in the land of Whimsy told exactly what kinds of jobs they have to do?

3. How many slaves are in Whimseyville?

4. Are there any dukes or earls in Whimseyville?

5. If you lived in Whimseyville what would you do in a day? A week? A year?

Presentation Page: the Suffix, **dom**

Review the root words. See how the suffix, **dom** changes the meaning of each word. These words are derivatives of the root words.

Select five derivatives from the list. Show how each was made below:

Root word	*plus*	**Suffix**	*equals*	**Derivative**
_____		_____		_____
_____		_____		_____
_____		_____		_____
_____		_____		_____
_____		_____		_____

Write a sentence with each of the derivatives using the suffix, **dom.**

_____

_____

_____

_____

_____

Answer the questions following the passage.

_____

_____

_____

_____

_____

Just for fun, try writing your own story using as many of the derivatives as possible.

Root words

auction - a public sale of items to the highest bidders

mountain - a large raised part of the earth

engine - a machine which uses energy to develop mechanical power

ballad - a song which tells a story

puppet - a small figure of a human or animal worked with strings

Derivatives (words made by adding the suffix, eer)

auctioneer - one who calls for bids at an auction

mountaineer - one who lives in the mountains

engineer - someone who works with engines

balladeer - someone who sings ballads

puppeteer - someone who makes a puppet talk and move

Read this passage and note how the derivatives are used. Answer the questions.

As the auction**eer** stepped up to the platform, a bearded man wearing jeans and a v-neck sweater entered the room. We were sure that this must be the mysterious mountain**eer** who lived in a cabin in the mountains outside of town. No one knew where he was from. Some say that he used to work as an engin**eer** for the railroad which no longer comes through this area. I've also heard that he was once a famous ballad**eer** whose songs were very popular, but he no longer sings. Others suspect that he was an actor and worked as a puppet**eer** in the early days of television. We were very curious as to what he might bid on at the auction. Perhaps this would give us a clue about his background.

1. Describe the man who entered the room as the auctioneer stepped up to the platform.

2. Could he be working for the railroad in town these days? Why?

3. Does anyone think that he might have been in the entertainment business?

4. Why do you guess that this mysterious man might have come to this auction?

Review the root words. See how the suffix, **eer** changes the meaning of each word.
These words are derivatives of the root words. Show how each derivative was made.

Root word	*plus*	Suffix	*equals*	Derivative
_____		_____		_____
_____		_____		_____
_____		_____		_____
_____		_____		_____
_____		_____		_____

Write a sentence with each of the derivatives using the suffix, **eer.**

_____

_____

_____

_____

_____

Answer the questions following the passage.

_____

_____

_____

_____

Just for fun, try writing your own story using as many of the derivatives as possible.

The Suffix, **hood** -- the rank, state or condition of something or someone

Root words

child - a young human being

man - an adult male human

woman - an adult female human

adult - a grown-up, mature person

boy - a male child

girl - a female child

parent - a mother or father

Derivatives (words made by adding the suffix, **hood**)

childhood - the state of being of a child, or young human being

manhood - the state of being a man

womanhood - the state of being a woman

adulthood - the state of being an adult, or grown-up, mature person

boyhood - the state of being a boy

girlhood - the state of being a girl

parenthood - the state of being a mother or father

Read this passage and note how the derivatives are used. Answer the questions.

> Child**hood** is a wonderful time of life. It's a time for enjoying, learning, playing, and imagining, while looking ahead to man**hood** or woman**hood**. Adult**hood** brings many privileges along with many responsibilities. An adult must work to make his or her community and country a better place. Adults must also be concerned with earning enough money to take care of themselves. This might be very hard sometimes, and an adult might wish to return to the carefree days of boy**hood** or girl**hood**. Parent**hood** brings even greater responsibilities. Parents must make a child's life happy so that the child can enjoy child**hood**. But parents must also teach some difficult lessons which will help youngsters grow to adult**hood**.

1. What kinds of things go on during one's childhood?

2. Why would a child look forward to adulthood?

3. Why might a child be a little afraid of manhood or womanhood?

4. Do you think that sometimes an adult might like to return to childhood? Why?

5. What are some things that parents must try to do?

Review the root words. See how the suffix, **hood** changes the meaning of each word. These words are derivatives of the root words.

Select five derivatives from the list. Show how each was made below:

Root word	*plus*	Suffix	*equals*	Derivative
_____		_____		_____
_____		_____		_____
_____		_____		_____
_____		_____		_____
_____		_____		_____

Write a sentence with each of the derivatives using the suffix, **hood.**

_____

_____

_____

_____

_____

_____

Answer the questions following the passage.

_____

_____

_____

_____

_____

Just for fun, try writing your own story using as many of the derivatives as possible.

The Suffix, **ible** -- being in a state of or able to be

Root words

horror - a strong feeling caused by something fearful or shocking

aud - a word part referring to hearing

sense - normal intelligence and judgment

intelligent - ability to understand

cred - a word part meaning to believe

permit - to allow

combust - a term which refers to burning

flex - to bend or change

Derivatives (words made by adding the suffix, **ible**)

horrible - in the state of horror

audible - able to be heard

sensible - using intelligence and good judgement

intelligible - able to be understood

credible - able to be believed

permissible - able to be done because it is allowed

combustible - able to be burned

flexible - able to be bent or changed

Read this passage and note how the derivatives are used. Answer the questions.

> No one in this neighborhood will ever forget the day the rocket ship from Planet Shark landed in the center of town. First, there was a horr**ible** roaring sound. Then we heard strange music which, at first, sounded loud, but grew so quiet that it was hardly aud**ible**. Then the Sharkians began to step out of the ship. At first the town people were frightened, but the Sharkians seemed to be sens**ible**, normal folks. They spoke our language very well and were quite intelligible. They said that they had heard of our town's fabulous ice cream, and they wanted to try some. They were right about the ice cream--it's incred**ible**! It's hard to believe such great ice cream can be found in a small town like ours. After they finished their ice cream, we asked to go aboard the ship, but the Sharkians said that this was not permiss**ible** because there were combust**ible** materials aboard. We said good-by, and invited them to come back again for more ice cream. They said that they would love to come. Since their work schedules are flex**ible**, they might be able to arrange it.

1. How did the neighborhood people know something unusual was happening the day the space ship landed?

2. Did the Sharkians come to threaten or injure the people?

3. Did the neighbors and the Sharkians have any communication problems? Why?

4. Did the neighbors get to go on board the space ship? Why?

5. Do you think the Sharkians might return some day? What makes you think so?

Review the root words. See how the suffix, **ible** changes the meaning of each word. These words are derivatives of the root words.

Select five derivatives from the list. Show how each was made below:

Root word	*plus*	Suffix	*equals*	Derivative
_____		_____		_____
_____		_____		_____
_____		_____		_____
_____		_____		_____
_____		_____		_____

Write a sentence with each of the derivatives using the suffix, **ible**.

_____

_____

_____

_____

_____

Answer the questions following the passage.

_____

_____

_____

_____

_____

Just for fun, try writing your own story using as many of the derivatives as possible.

Root words

natural - concerned with nature

biology - the study of life

botany - the study of plants

column - a feature article appearing regularly in a newspaper

tour - a trip for sightseeing

motor - anything that produces motion

science - the study of something

Derivatives (words made by adding the suffix, **ist**)

naturalist - one who works with nature

biologist - a specialist in life science

botanist - a specialist in plant live

columnist - someone who writes a column

tourist - someone who is traveling and sightseeing

motorist - one who drives a motorized vehicle

scientist - someone who specializes in a scientific field

Read this passage and note how the derivatives are used. Answer the questions.

There is a most unusual plant growing in the center of our town. One day it just appeared. No one planted it. At first we thought it was a weed, but no one seems to be able to kill it or remove it. The naturalists from the museum are trying to learn about this plant. They've called biologists and botanists from all over, but, so far, no one can recall ever seeing anything like it. A newspaper columnist wrote a story about the plant, and now tourists are starting to come to town to see it. Traffic around the square gets tied up sometimes because motorists stop their cars and look. Scientists are studying the plant and might have learned something; however, they have not reported anything to us. Meanwhile we imagine all kinds of different things. Maybe it will grow to be as tall as Jack's beanstalk and allow us to climb to a fantastic new land!

1.   Where did the strange plant come from?

2.   How did the people conclude that the plant was not a weed?

3.   Who has studied the plant so far? What did they find out?

4.   What do some people imagine that the plant might be?

5.   What would you imagine about the plant?

Review the root words. See how the suffix, **ist** changes the meaning of each word.
These words are derivatives of the root words.

Select five derivatives from the list. Show how each was made below:

Root word	*plus*	**Suffix**	*equals*	**Derivative**
_____		_____		_____
_____		_____		_____
_____		_____		_____
_____		_____		_____
_____		_____		_____

Write a sentence with each of the derivatives using the suffix, **ist**.

_____

_____

_____

_____

_____

Answer the questions following the passage.

_____

_____

_____

_____

_____

Just for fun, try writing your own story using as many of the derivatives as possible.

The Suffix, **ize** -- to act upon or make

Root words

real - actual, not artificial or fake

economy - referring to money or finance

fertile - producing plentifully or abundantly

colony - a community of individuals with something in common

symbol - an object used to represent an idea

Derivatives (words made by adding the suffix, ize)

realize - to become real

economize - to manage resources carefully

fertilize - to cause something to become fertile

colonize - to form a colony

symbolize - to represent an idea

Read this passage and note how the derivatives are used. Answer the questions.

When the early settlers arrived in the new land, they realized a dream. They had their own farms and were free to express their ideas as they chose. They had very little food, other supplies, and resources and had to economize in many ways. They grew their own fruits and vegetables, and they sometimes fertilized the soil with scraps so that nothing would be wasted. All of the colonists were loyal to each other and to the new land. Colonization had helped to make them strong and very proud. They built a monument in the center of their new village to symbolize their loyalty to their community.

1. What did the settlers enjoy about their new land?

2. How did they manage to get along with few supplies and very little food?

3. What was the colonists' attitude toward one another?

4. What proof is there that the colonists loved their new way of life?

Review the root words. See how the suffix, **ize** changes the meaning of each word.
These words are derivatives of the root words. Show how each derivative was made.

Root word	*plus*	**Suffix**	*equals*	**Derivative**
_____		_____		_____
_____		_____		_____
_____		_____		_____
_____		_____		_____
_____		_____		_____

Write a sentence with each of the derivatives using the suffix, **ize**.

_____

_____

_____

_____

_____

Answer the questions following the passage.

_____

_____

_____

_____

Just for fun, try writing your own story using as many of the derivatives as possible.

Root words	**Derivatives** (words made by adding the suffix, **less**)
home - the place where one lives	**homeless** - without a place to live
power - strength or influence	**powerless** - without strength or influence
worth - value	**worthless** - having no value
hope - feeling that what is wanted will happen	**hopeless** - without hope
help - assistance or aid in improving something	**helpless** - without aid or assistance to improve something
tired - weary or exhausted	**tireless** - without weariness or exhaustion
use - function	**useless** - without function
price - amount of money needed to buy something	**priceless** - not having a specified dollar value
purpose - reason for being or for doing something	**purposeless** - without reason for being or doing

Read this passage and note how the derivatives are used. Answer the questions.

> The citizens of Buena Vista, the city where I live, are working hard to help people who have no jobs or no place to live. Many of these home**less** people had once worked in responsible jobs. But some big companies closed the factories where these people worked, and the workers were power**less** to change this. Now these people feel worth**less** and hope**less**. They're help**less** because they don't have money to move to a town where they might find jobs.
>
> Our neighbors feel that we must work tire**less**ly to find ways for these home**less**, unemployed people to contribute their skills and energy to make our city a better place. No person is use**less**. Everyone has a mind which is a price**less** treasure. No person's life and ideas are purpose**less**. I'm proud to live in a city where we know that each of our citizens is an important person.

1. Why do some people become homeless when they lose their jobs?

2. Are the citizens of Buena Vista satisfied with everything in their city the way it is today?

3. Why do some people lose their jobs?

4. Why do the citizens of Buena Vista think their city will become better if the people with no jobs can find work?

5. How does the person writing this feel about his or her town? Why?

Review the root words. See how the suffix, **less** changes the meaning of each word. These words are derivatives of the root words.

Select five derivatives from the list. Show how each was made below:

Root word	*plus*	**Suffix**	*equals*	**Derivative**
_____		_____		_____
_____		_____		_____
_____		_____		_____
_____		_____		_____
_____		_____		_____

Write a sentence with each of the derivatives using the suffix, **less**.

_____

_____

_____

_____

_____

Answer the questions following the passage.

_____

_____

_____

_____

_____

Just for fun, try writing your own story using as many of the derivatives as possible.

The Suffix, **mate** -- partner, associate, someone with whom you do something together

Root words

play - fun, amusement

class - a group of people who are all the same in some way

team - a group of people working together

bunk - a sleeping place

ship - a large vessel navigating deep water

room - an interior space enclosed by walls

office - a place for carrying on business affairs

Derivatives (words made by adding the suffix, **mate**)

playmate - someone to have fun with

classmate - a fellow member in one's class

teammate - a fellow member of a team

bunkmate - someone who shares one's sleeping quarters

shipmate - a fellow sailor

roommate - someone who shares one's room

officemate - someone who shares one's office

Read this passage and note how the derivatives are used. Answer the questions.

When Lynn leaves town next month, Sara will miss her best friend. Sara and Lynn have been friends almost all their lives. They were play**mate**s when they were children. They were class**mate**s throughout elementary school and team**mate**s on the school soccer team for years. They went to the same camp each summer for several years and were always bunk**mate**s. They loved to sail on the lake near their homes. They talked of growing up and some day being ship**mate**s in the Navy!

Instead, they went to college where they were room**mate**s. After graduating from law school, they found a small office where they were office**mate**s for several years. After raising their families, Sara became interested in business law and Lynn went into local politics. Lynn proved to be an excellent leader. In the last election she was elected to the United States Congress. Sara will miss Lynn when she leaves for Washington next month but is very proud and happy for her friend.

1. For how long have Sara and Lynn been friends?

2. Did they enjoy sports?

3. What careers were Sara and Lynn involved in?

4. Did Sara and Lynn do the same job after they raised their families as they did before raising their families?

5. What is Lynn's new job? How long will she have this job?

Review the root words. See how the suffix, **mate** changes the meaning of each word. These words are derivatives of the root words.

Select five derivatives from the list. Show how each was made below:

Root word	*plus*	Suffix	*equals*	Derivative
_____		_____		_____
_____		_____		_____
_____		_____		_____
_____		_____		_____
_____		_____		_____

Write a sentence with each of the derivatives using the suffix, **mate**.

_____

_____

_____

_____

_____

Answer the questions following the passage.

_____

_____

_____

_____

_____

Just for fun, try writing your own story using as many of the derivatives as possible.

Root words

shatter - to break into many pieces

rust - a reddish-brown coating formed on iron or steel during exposure to air and moisture

weather - the condition of the atmosphere with regard to air and moisture

fire - something burning

child - a young human

Derivatives (words made by adding the suffix, **proof**)

shatterproof - safe from breaking into many pieces

rustproof - safe from developing rust

weatherproof - protected against damaging weather

fireproof - safe from fire

childproof - safe from damage which might be caused by a child

Read this passage and note how the derivatives are used. Answer the questions.

> Mom and Dad decided to do something about all the dishes that get broken at our house. They sent for some new dishes guaranteed to be the toughest ever made. They're shatter**proof**; so, if we drop a dish or cup, it won't break and get little pieces of glass all over. They're rust**proof** because they're made of a strong plastic material. They are completely weather**proof**, thus, they won't warp, crack, or fade if they're left out in the sun. They won't crack if they get too hot or cold. Even if there's a fire, the dishes won't be damaged because they're fire**proof**. They're about as child**proof** as they could be. They're guaranteed to be safe from kids!
>
> I wish that the people who make those dishes would start making pants and shirts. It would save me a lot of trouble if my clothes were child**proof**!

1. Why did the writer's parents order these new dishes?

2. What will happen to one of the new dishes if it's dropped on cement?

3. Will these dishes be destroyed in a fire?

4. What might be more easily damaged, these dishes or children's clothes? Why?

Review the root words. See how the suffix, **proof** changes the meaning of each word.
These words are derivatives of the root words. Show how each derivative was made.

Select five derivatives from the list. Show how each was made below:

Root word	*plus*	Suffix	*equals*	Derivative
_____		_____		_____
_____		_____		_____
_____		_____		_____
_____		_____		_____
_____		_____		_____

Write a sentence with each of the derivatives using the suffix, **proof.**

_____

_____

_____

_____

_____

Answer the questions following the passage.

_____

_____

_____

_____

Just for fun, try writing your own story using as many of the derivatives as possible.

The Suffix, **ward** -- in the direction of

Root words

up -to, in or on a higher place or level

down - to, in or on a lower place or level

home - the place where one lives

lee- shelter from the wind

wind -air in motion

after - later

Derivatives (words made by adding the suffix, **ward**)

upward - in a higher direction

downward - in a lower direction

homeward - toward the place where one lives

leeward - away from the wind

windward - toward the wind

afterward - toward a later time

Read this passage and note how the derivatives are used. Answer the questions.

The climbers had finally reached the summit of the highest mountain in the world. They were happy to have reached this goal. They looked up**ward** and saw only the sky. Looking down**ward** they saw snow-covered mountain peaks and lots of clouds. Now, they must head home**ward**. They will climb down the lee**ward** side of the mountain because they would be too uncomfortable climbing down the wind**ward** side. After**ward**, they will write a book about their adventure.

1. What had the climbers' goal been? Did they reach their goal?

2. What could they see from where they stood?

3. Could they see their friends and their homes which were at the foot of the mountain? Why?

4. What will they do in order to make their trip back down the mountain as comfortable as possible?

5. What do you think are some of the adventures that they might write about in their book?

Review the root words. See how the suffix, **ward** changes the meaning of each word.
These words are derivatives of the root words.

Select five derivatives from the list. Show how each was made below:

Root word	*plus*	**Suffix**	*equals*	**Derivative**
_____		_____		_____
_____		_____		_____
_____		_____		_____
_____		_____		_____
_____		_____		_____

Write a sentence with each of the derivatives using the suffix, **ward**.

_____

_____

_____

_____

_____

Answer the questions following the passage.

_____

_____

_____

_____

_____

Just for fun, try writing your own story using as many of the derivatives as possible.

The Suffix, **work** -- the product or result of some type of labor or skill

Root words

art - creativity or skill

basket - a container made of interwoven cane, wood strips, or other materials

metal - a hard shiny material which can conduct heat and electricity

leather - animal skin treated with tannic acid

team - a group of individuals working toward a common goal

house - a structure built to be lived in

school - a place of learning

handy - skilled use of one's hands

Derivatives (words made by adding the suffix, **work**)

artwork - products created and produced using one's skill

basketwork - the skill and products involved in making woven containers

metalwork - products skillfully made out of metal

leatherwork - products skillfully made out of leather

teamwork - working together in a group toward reaching a goal

housework - skills and effort necessary to keep a house in order

schoolwork - skills and effort necessary to support learning at school

handiwork - products made by hand

Read this passage and note how the derivatives are used. Answer the questions.

The Swansons would love to earn their living by selling their artwork. They had always wanted to open a craft shop where they could sell the things which they make. Mr. Swanson and eleven-year-old Samantha weave beautiful baskets. Their basketwork is well-known in the area. Mrs. Swanson is a painter whose artwork is very beautiful. Fifteen-year-old Chris does fine metalwork and makes jewelry. He is also very skilled at leatherwork. Everyone in town admires his hand-tooled belts. At the town craft fair last spring even the mayor bought one for herself!

They will open their shop this summer. Their business should be a success because their products are excellent, and they are willing to work hard. It will take a lot of special efforts for everyone and teamwork for the family. Housework and schoolwork must come first. But they are proud of their handiwork and are excited and happy about the new business.

---

1. What are some of the special talents of the Swanson family?

2. How do the Swansons plan to sell their handiwork? What are some other ways that talented people sell the things that they make?

3. Do you think their business will be a success? Why?

4. What responsibilities do the family members have besides the responsibilities at the craft shop?

Review the root words. See how the suffix, **work** changes the meaning of each word. These words are derivatives of the root words.

Select five derivatives from the list. Show how each was made below:

Root word	*plus*	**Suffix**	*equals*	**Derivative**
_____		_____		_____
_____		_____		_____
_____		_____		_____
_____		_____		_____
_____		_____		_____

Write a sentence with each of the derivatives using the suffix, **work**.

_____

_____

_____

_____

_____

Answer the questions following the passage.

_____

_____

_____

_____

Just for fun, try writing your own story using as many of the derivatives as possible.

The suffix, **mate** means partner or someone who shares something with others. Teammates are people who are on a team together. There are many different kinds of teams. Following is a list of some of them. Use this list of teams to fill in the blank in each sentence.

swim	golf	football	crew	debate	rescue	gymnastics
baseball	race car	tennis	surgical	hockey	track	basketball

1. The _____ teammates were talking about field goals, touchdowns, and a quarterback.

2. The _____ teammates were talking about strike outs, a catcher's mitt, and the World Series.

3. The _____ teammates were talking about a goalie, a stick, and a puck.

4. The _____ teammates were talking about the center, free throws, and the fowl line.

5. The _____ teammates were talking about a balance beam, vault, and floor exercises.

6. The _____ teammates were talking about the tee, a putter, and a nine-iron.

7. The _____ teammates were talking about tires, a carburetor, and pit stops.

8. The _____ teammates were talking about backstrokes, free style strokes, and butterfly strokes.

9. The _____ teammates were talking about the net, racquets, and a match.

10. The _____ teammates were talking about a scalpel, a heart monitor, and the operating room.

11. The _____ teammates were talking abut oars, the stroke, and the coxswain.

12. The _____ teammates were talking about meters, sprints, and relays.

13. The _____ teammates were talking about the podium, the speakers, and note cards.

14. The _____ teammates were talking about ropes, a two-way radio, and an airlift.

The suffix, **work** means the work, labor, or a product of certain craftspeople.

■ Below is a list of types of craftsmanship and a list of products which might be made by them. Write the correct type of craftsmanship on the line after each product.

Types of craftsmanship

artwork	leatherwork	woodwork
metalwork	glasswork	basketwork

Product

purse	_____	an oil painting	_____
a silver tray	_____	a water color painting	_____
a bread basket	_____	a wooden jewelry box	_____
a pewter bowl	_____	a railing	_____
a delicate glass figure	_____	a belt	_____
a bookshelf	_____	a metal sculpture	_____

■ Complete the following sentences using these words ending with the suffix, **work**.

homework	teamwork	paperwork	roadwork
housework	guesswork	clockwork	patchwork

1. Schoolwork which is done at home is called _____ .

2. Many people who work spend a lot of time filling out forms, writing reports, and filing papers. Often these people complain about having so much _____ that they can't do their jobs!

3. The coach always tells us that our win/loss record depends on practice and _____ .

4. We have to take a detour because the workers are doing some _____ along our route home.

5. Our whole family helps get the _____ done since Mom went to work.

6. When we work with such valuable materials, we must be very sure and careful. There is no room for _____ .

7. "It went like _____," is an expression meaning that everything moved along as expected.

8. Grandma made a beautiful _____ quilt.

The prefix **pre** means before. The prefix **post** means after.

When a country is at war and the battles take place inside that country, many things are destroyed. Buildings and towns are sometimes reconstructed afterwards, but the original features are often lost forever. Buildings and special structures which might have stood for centuries can be destroyed in minutes.

■ Below is a list of statements about Europe before and after World War II, which took place between 1939 and 1945. Many World War II battles were fought in Europe. On the line following each statement indicate whether this statement probably refers to a *prewar* or a *postwar* fact.

1. Hundreds of priceless works of art are on display at a museum build in the 12th Century. This museum has never been disturbed and looks very much like it did when it was built.

_____

2. Most of the paintings in the museum mentioned above have been destroyed; fewer than 100 remain.

_____

3. A modern train system runs throughout the city. This system was completed in the 1960s.

_____

4. People travel on the train to visit relatives in another town. They don't know that this train will some day carry thousands of people to their death in concentration camps.

_____

5. A world-famous opera house stands in the center of a city. The seats are covered with velvet and trimmed with gold. Members of royal families have sat in these seats for centuries enjoying the opera.

_____

6. As the curtain rose in the opera house, TV cameras panned the audience seated in seats covered with a man-made fabric which looked like velvet.

_____

The terms *preop* and *postop* are used by doctors and nurses referring to circumstances before (preop) and after (postop) an operation. Ed had his appendix removed last week. The following sentences refer to events that took place around the time of the operation.

■ On the line following each sentence write the word *preop* or *postop* indicating whether each event might have taken place before or after the operation.

Ed noticed a pain in his side, but thought it might be a pulled muscle. He was wrong. His appendix was beginning to become inflamed.

_____

Ed stayed in the recovery room until he awoke from the anesthetic.

_____

A nurse gave Ed a pill to relax him before he received the anesthetic.

_____

The stitches were removed.

_____

Ed cannot walk up steps for several days.

_____

The prefix, **sub** means below or beneath. Marine refers to water. Therefore, a submarine is a vessel which can travel below water. These unique ships can travel above the water, as any ship could. But they can also travel just below or deeply below the surface of the sea. Submarines have many special features and uses.

■ Fill in the blanks below using the words, *submarine*, *beneath*, *below*, or *above*.

A _____ is used as a warship because it cannot easily be detected by enemy ships. It is difficult to detect because it travels _____ the water.

Submarines are sometimes used for rescuing persons or objects from ships which have sunk. Ordinary steamships could not do this because they cannot travel _____ the surface of the water.

While cruising just beneath the water a _____ officer can view the surroundings above the surface using a periscope. A periscope is a long tube containing lenses and prisms which extends several feet upward from inside the submarine. When a sailor is in a submarine traveling just _____ the water, he or she can use the periscope to see things _____ the water.

Thirty-two degrees Fahrenheit is the point at which water freezes. When the temperature of the air reaches 32°F, we say that it is *freezing*. If it falls below 32°F we say that it is below freezing or *subfreezing*.

■ Following is a list of temperatures for some days in a Midwestern city last year. Write *above freezing* or *subfreezing* on the line next to the date and temperature. If it is a subfreezing temperature, indicate how many degrees below freezing the temperature was.

Date	Temperature	
January 9	28° F	_____
January 20	10° F	_____
February 1	30° F	_____
February 14	0° F	_____
February 15	-2° F	_____
March 1	37° F	_____

When a house is built, a general contractor is usually in charge of the complete job. The person who wants to have the house built arranges the design and decorating with the general contractor who supervises the construction. The contractor, then, hires subcontractors to do special jobs.

■ Here are a list of subcontractors and a list of jobs that need to be done. Try to match the subcontractor to the special job which he or she might do as a new house is built.

an electrical subcontractor	nail shingles on
a plumbing subcontractor	pour the foundation
a carpenter	install bathroom fixtures
a bricklayer	run wires throughout the house
a roofing subcontractor	smooth the wall surfaces
a plasterer	build a fireplace
a cement subcontractor	build the wood frame of the house

The suffix, **age** means an amount or collection of something. Each word in the column on the left was derived by adding the suffix, **age** to a root word. Match each word in the left column with the best definition in the right column.

acreage	an amount of miles
baggage	the amount of land measured in acres
coinage	a collection of bags
leakage	an amount of coins
mileage	the amount that something might shrink
wattage	a collection of something which has leaked
sewage	an amount of electrical power measured in watts
shrinkage	an amount of materials which have entered a sewer

■ Complete the following sentences using the words above.

1. These jeans are guaranteed against _____ after they are washed.

2. The farmer sold off some of the _____ from the huge farm.

3. The health department was concerned when untreated _____ emptied into the lake where people swim.

4. The total _____ needed for all of the electric appliances is more than this house has available.

5. The _____ from the water pipe formed a large puddle behind the house.

6. The manager carried the paper money to the bank, but the _____ was delivered by truck.

7. Newer cars have improved gas _____.

8. I put my suitcase in the _____ compartment of the train.

■ Keeping in mind that the larger a vehicle, the fewer miles per gallon of fuel possible, match the vehicle on the left with the estimated mileage on the right.

a large motorcycle	6 gallons per mile
a moving van	up to 28 mpg
a small four-cylinder car	up to 12 mpg
a large eight-cylinder car	up to 100 mpg
a small motorcycle	5 or 6 mpg
a jumbo jet	up to 65 mpg

The suffix **ant** means someone who or something which. For example, a servant is someone who serves a person, a nation, or a cause. A pollutant is something that pollutes the environment.

Has your family ever received mail addressed to Occupant, followed by your address? When this happens, it means that someone wants to get a message to whomever lives at your address and is occupying your house at the time.

■ Just for fun, look at the envelopes below; each is addressed to an occupant at a particular address. Look at the return address on the envelope and, using your imagination, decide who or what type of person might be the occupant.

J&M Medical Supplies
Los Angeles, CA
 	
        Occupant
        7901 E. 4th St.
        Pittsburgh, PA
	Ace Piano Tuners, Inc.
	Cleveland, OH
	
	        Occupant
	        6690 Tumbleweed Dr.
	        Dallas, TX

Joe Smith's
Easels & Brushes
New York, NY
 	
        Occupant
        3908 Sunnyview Ave.
        Phoenix, AZ
	Wholesale Only Cosmetics
	Chicago, IL
	
	        Occupant
	        4411 Pilgrim Trail
	        Boston, MA

Dr. M. Tas
Veterinarian
Indianapolis, IN
 	
        Occupant
        2020 Monument Blvd.
        Washington, DC
	Star Talent Agency
	Hollywood, CA
	
	        Occupant
	        1786 Magnolia St.
	        Mobile, AL

Ken's Fitness Center
Louisville, KY
 	
        Occupant
        7634 Seaside Rd.
        San Diego, CA
	Interface Software Co.
	Houston, TX
	
	        Occupant
	        4207 Bronco Rd.
	        Laramie, WY

The prefix, **trans** means over or across. The term, *port* comes from a Latin word meaning to carry. Transport, therefore, means to carry something or someone over or across a space.

■ Complete the following sentences with the correct means of transportation:

taxi	school bus	junk	camel
bicycle	carrier pigeon	jet plane	elephant
horse	submarine	aircraft carrier	chariot
wheelchair	golf cart	helicopter	dump truck
moving van	subway	freight train	rocket ship

1. The woman drove her _____ around the course so that she would not have to carry her clubs.

2. The king rode through the center of the village in a horse-driven _____.

3. I'll have to call a _____ to take me to the airport, since I have so much luggage.

4. The sheik rode across the desert on a _____. This is not an unusual means of transportation in this part of the world.

5. When I go to New York City, I ride under the streets on the _____

6. Dad ordered a load of topsoil for the garden, and it was delivered in a _____.

7. Every morning the _____ transports my friends and me to school.

8. The prisoner of war wrote small messages and sent them to his countrymen by _____ because he could not leave the prison camp or use the mail or telephone.

9. A _____ is the fastest means of transportation available to most people in our country.

10. Grandma has trouble walking but enjoys going around the shopping mall in a _____.

11. The accident victims were transported to the hospital by medical _____ because it was too far to go by ambulance.

12. Some manufacturing companies transport their products and materials by _____ because it is more convenient and economical than transporting them by truck.

13. Until I'm old enough to drive, my feet and my _____ will be my most important means of transportation.

14. The Chinese sailors sailed across the bay in a type of vessel used by Chinese people for many generations called a _____.

15. The rancher rode a _____ as she rounded up the herd of cattle.

16. Our furniture was transported by a _____ when we moved from Oregon to Florida.

17. The Navy uses _____ during wartime because they cannot be seen by enemy sailors.

18. In India the _____ is a means of transportation.

19. The life squad transported our neighbor to the hospital by _____ when he suffered from chest pains.

20. The fighter plane landed on an _____ which was in the Pacific Ocean.

The suffixes, **dom** and **hood** mean being; manhood means being a man; freedom means being free.

■ Below are several sentences, each telling of a person. On the line following each sentence write a word from the list below which might be associated with the person in the sentence.

childhood	adulthood	manhood
womanhood	freedom	babyhood
bachelorhood	stardom	knighthood
sisterhood	priesthood	wisdom

1. Larry is very smart and uses good judgement. _____

2. Katie is an adult female. _____

3. Sir Robert wore a suit of armor and carried a sword. _____

4. Mark and Kevin are four-year-old twins. _____

5. Father George performs religious ceremonies. _____

6. The famous singer gives concerts all over the country. It is hard to _____ get tickets because the concerts are usually sold out.

7. Sally has four older and two younger brothers. _____

8. Mike is a 28-year-old unmarried man. _____

9. Beth lives in a country where all the citizens are allowed to speak _____ and write about anything they wish.

10. All the teachers on the faculty are at least 22 years old. _____

11. Sue was born just two days ago. _____

12. Greg can't find anything to do. It seems like this day is lasting _____ forever!

13. Mark is an adult male member of the human species. _____

The prefixes, **im** and **in** mean not. Impossible means not possible; impolite means not polite.

■ Use these words to complete the sentences below.

impolite	inattentive	incorrect
inaudible	invisible	inactive
impure	independent	impossible

1. There is no way that this job can be done. It is an _____ job.

2. The girls were talking to each other while the guest speaker was giving her speech. What word describes this rude behavior? _____

3. When something can neither be seen nor heard it is both _____ and _____.

4. In 1776, our country became an _____ nation. We celebrate Independence Day on July 4th.

5. Bill was not paying attention when the assignment was given. Because he was _____, he did not know what to do for homework that night.

6. The river has been polluted with chemicals from nearby factories for many years. The citizens can not use the river water in their homes because it is _____. In order to get fresh water, the town will activate a well which was _____ for many years.

7. Bob received 80% on his spelling test. Out of ten words, eight were right, but two were _____.

■ Semi means half or partly. If chocolate candy is not as sweet as we expect, but it is not really bitter either, we might say the chocolate is semi-sweet. Use your imagination. Using the prefix **semi**, make up words to finish these sentences.

1. Marcy tried to pay attention during the film. She watched most of it, but toward the end she started thinking of what she might wear to the party that night. She was not really inattentive; she was only _____.

2. Tom could almost, but not quite, see the harbor through the fog. The harbor was _____ to him.

3. The radio was playing so softly that we could only slightly hear it when we strained to listen. The radio was not fully audible, only _____.

The suffix, **ward** means in the direction of. We often hear the phrase "upward direction" or "downward direction." These phrases might refer to actual objects moving upward or downward like airplanes or helicopters. Sometimes we use the terms upward and downward to refer to things that we can't really see, rather things we just think about.

When many people become involved or interested in something or begin to like or buy a certain type of product or act in a certain way, we refer to this as a trend. When interest or sales grow, we say that the trend is moving upward. When sales or interest shrinks or diminishes, we say that the trend is moving downward.

■ Practice expressing this idea as you look at this graph which tells of the sales of an imaginary product called a *yebbit*. The numbers on the left of the graph tell the number of yebbits sold, counting by 10's as you move upward. The points along the bottom of the graph refer to the months of the year. You can see that 10 yebbits were sold in January, and 30 were sold in February.

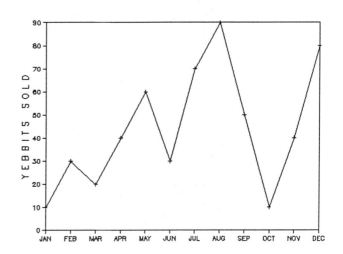

■ Use the following sentence to tell whether there was an upward or downward trend in the sale of yebbits for the months, March through December. "There was an _(upward or downward)_ trend in the sale of yebbits in _(month)_."

■ Just for fun, discuss with teachers or parents areas suggested below or discuss other areas where we have seen upward or downward trends in interest or sales in the past few years. Think about why these trends might have occurred as they did.

compact cars

stock prices

country music

salad bars

length of hair

frozen yogurt

smoking

exercise

■ Complete the sentences following the definitions of the prefixes, **inter**, **intra** and **co**.

The prefix, **inter** means among or between.

Interstate means between or among _____.

International means between or among many _____.

Interplanetary means between or among many _____.

Interdepartmental means between or among many _____.

Intercommunication means _____ between many persons (**inter**com is a shorter way of saying **inter**communication).

The prefix, **intra** means within one body, geographic area, and so forth.

Intrastate means within one _____.

Intravenous means within the _____ of the body.

Intramural means within the _____ of a building (mural means wall).

The prefix **co** means together with.

Cooperate means to operate or work _____.

Coexist means two or more people or groups exist _____.

■ Complete the following sentences using words which contain the prefixes **inter**, **intra**, and **co**.

1. _____ 75 is a highway which runs through Florida, Alabama, Georgia, Tennessee, Kentucky, Ohio, and Michigan.

2. The _____ Red Cross serves victims of disasters in many countries.

3. The new ultramodern space station will include high-tech _____ systems allowing someone on Earth to talk to someone on Mars.

4. Each year an _____ education conference is held in the state capital. Teachers from all over this state attend.

5. An important _____ meeting was called and all department managers had to be present.

6. Because the man could not swallow, the doctors ordered an _____ feeding. The "IV" contained nourishment along with medicine.

7. The principal announced a free day over the _____.

■ Explain what is meant by the phrase, *international cooperation*.

_____

■ What does *peaceful coexistence between nations* mean?

_____

The prefix, **mis** means wrong. The prefix, **re** means again. Following is a list of words containing these prefixes. Indicate which of these words might best be associated with the following sentences. Write the word on the line following the sentence.

misprint	rewrite
misuse	retake
mispronounce	reuse
misspell	restate
misunderstood	reprint
misread	reorder
misplace	recalculate
miscalculate	relabel
mislabel	refile
misfile	reread

1. Jim knew that he had his keys in his hands a moment ago, but he just can't find them now! _____

2. The instructions were very complicated, so I made several errors as I tried to do the project. _____

3. Dad estimated that the trip would take about 36 hours, but he didn't allow enough time for meals and rest. We arrived about 7 hours late. _____

4. The name appearing on my locker was Kevan. My name is Kevin. _____

5. Mom said that I should save my lunch bag from today because she can put my lunch in this same bag tomorrow. _____

6. Kelly's senior pictures turned out awful. She'll return to the photographer next Thursday. _____

■ The following sentences each have two blanks. Try to fill in one of the blanks in each sentence with a word beginning with **mis**, the other blank with a word beginning with **re**.

1. The report was _____ in the drawer under *expenses* and must be _____ under *earnings*.

2. The clerk _____ all of the jars of jelly. No one could tell what kind of jelly was in each jar. He had to stay after work for several hours to _____ them.

3. The salesman _____ the total cost of my supplies and gave me the wrong change. I asked him to _____ the amount so that he would see that he owed me money.

4. The clerk _____ some items from our order and so he had to _____ them.

5. I _____ the directions and got lost. When I _____ them, I realized that I had gotten off at the wrong exit.

6. There was a _____ in our store's ad in the paper this morning. The editor apologized and said she would _____ the ad free of charge in tomorrow's paper.

7. The teacher _____ some of the names and places on the class list, so he immediately _____ them.

8. Because the report was sloppy and had many _____ words, the teacher told Sara to _____ it.

9. I failed the test because I'd _____ the instructions. The teacher was nice enough to let me _____ the test the next day.

10. The students _____ the paint brushes in art class this morning. Unfortunately, they were damaged and can never be _____.

The prefix, **tele** means far. Telecommunications refers to means of communication over distances using electronic devices.

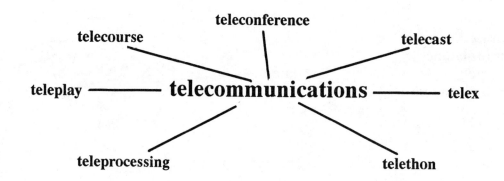

telecourse - a high school or college course taught over television

teleconference - a conference of individuals in different locations

telex - a typewriter using a telephone dial to establish communication

telecast - to broadcast by television

teleplay - a play written and produced for viewing on television

teleprocessing - data processing using computer terminals

telethon - a lengthy broadcast seeking support for a cause (*tele* means far, mara*thon* means long)

■ Use the words above to complete the following sentences.

1. We watched a twelve-hour _____ where famous performers appeared and asked for money to buy homes for homeless people.

2. Bret started his college education by taking a _____ in chemistry.

3. The newest machine in my mom's high-tech office is a _____. Her secretary likes it much better than typing messages on the old typewriter and sending them by mail.

4. The creative young playwright has just completed his first _____, which will be appear this fall.

5. There will be an extended _____ about the hostages at 11:30 P.M., following the news.

6. The managers were required to be in their offices by 8:00 A.M., so that they could all take part in the _____.

7. Data will be _____ and stored on computer discs.

Activity Page: the Prefix, **tele**

The suffix, **ize** means to act upon or to make. A symbol is an object or a printed mark which stands for or represents something. When a symbol symbolizes an idea, this symbol has been made to, designed for, or has come to be associated or connected with the idea in people's minds.

■ Following are 16 symbols and the idea which each symbolizes. Say a sentence telling why you think each symbol represents this idea and/or where a particular symbol might appear.

peace	poison
love	Something associated with Ireland
(white flag) surrender	water
no smoking	Republican Party
Democratic Party	no trucks allowed
music	time out
hospital	airport
campground	food

The suffix, **ist** means doer or performer. A tourist is someone who tours or travels in order to see interesting places and things. A tourist attraction is a special place event, natural setting, a man-made structure, or entertainment center where tourists like to go.

■ Following is a list of tourist attractions (left column) and a list of states (right column). Match each tourist attraction with the state in which it is located. Try to say or write a sentence telling why tourists like each of these places.

Statue of Liberty	New York
Houston Space Center	South Dakota
Henry Ford Museum	Arizona
Grand Canyon	Texas
U.S.S. Constitution	Florida
Liberty Bell	Kentucky
EPCOT Center	California
Rose Bowl Parade	Washington D.C.
Mammoth Cave	New York
U.S. Mint	Pennsylvania
Niagara Falls	Massachusetts
Mount Rushmore	Michigan

■ Say or write a sentence telling why a tourist might need the following things:

road map

luggage

reservations

travelers' checks

guide book

comfortable shoes

umbrella

sunglasses

lots of time

Activity Page: the Suffix, **ist**

The suffix, **able** means able to be.The word, *reasonable* means able to reason or to act in a sensible way or to do what's normally expected.

■ Sometimes, we think that people, circumstances, or rules are reasonable; sometimes we think they are unreasonable. Discuss the following ideas. Say what you think is reasonable or unreasonable, and why you think so.

1. **Homework assignments**. What is the reason for homework? What is a reasonable amount of time to spend working on homework each day?

2. **Speed limits**. What is a reasonable highway speed? What is a reasonable speed limit for driving through neighborhoods? Is it reasonable for the government to set speed limits?

3. **Prices**. Sometimes many facts must be considered when we try to determine if a price is reasonable or not. For example, a traveling salesperson use a car and travel far, drive for long hours, maintain a schedule, and keep products in the car. This salesperson might need a more expensive car than a student who wants to drive to school instead of riding the bus. Remembering this, think about what a reasonable price would be for: a businessperson to pay for a <u>suit</u>, a student to pay for a <u>pair of jeans</u>, or anyone to pay for a <u>candy bar</u>, a <u>record</u>, a <u>lamp</u>, a <u>speeding ticket</u>?

4. **Curfew**. This is the time that one is required by law to be indoors at night. Is it reasonable for families to set curfews for children and teen-agers? Is it reasonable for cities to set curfews for those below a certain age?

5. **Responsibilities at home**. What are some reasonable duties and responsibilities around home for a 6-year-old, an 8-year-old, a 10-year-old, or a 14-year old?

The suffix, **ible** also means able to be, and is used the same way as the suffix, **able**, only in different words. A word which we hear quite often these days is incredible. When we look at the parts of this word, we can understand it better:

In means not. The term, **cred** means believe. The suffix, **ible** means able to be.

So, the word incredible means not able to be believed; another way of saying unbelievable.

■ Just for fun, think of something that would be incredible in each of these categories. Describe your idea of what would be an incredible.

sports car	dessert	
birthday present	hair style	
sports event	teacher	
Halloween costume	vacation	
homework assignment	pet	

The prefix, **en** means to make or to put something into a particular situation. Some of the animals living today are considered to be endangered species because scientists are afraid that soon they will no longer be living on this planet.

Some of these animals' homelands have been destroyed by people trying to find minerals and other resources. Some animals' homes have been turned into towns or recreation areas. In some cases, the food which some of these animals had depended upon has become very scarce, and the endangered animals might not have enough to eat. Also, water and air pollution have damaged the living environments and breeding places of some endangered animals. Sometimes, too, people have hunted and killed animals so that they can sell parts of their bodies. The ivory from elephants' tusks is valuable, and elephants have been hunted for that reason.

■ Did you know that these animals are members of endangered species?

Mammals

Bobcat	Cheetah	Asian elephant	Gorilla
Leopard	Asiatic lion	Giant panda	Tiger
Gray whale	Mountain zebra	Grizzly bear	Ocelot
Florida panther	Utah prairie dog	Red wolf	

Birds

California condor	Whooping crane	Bald eagle
West African ostrich	Golden parakeet	Australian parrot

Reptiles

American alligator

American crocodile

Fish

Yaqui catfish

Gila trout

■ Think about and discuss some of these ideas:

Could laws be made to protect some endangered species?

How does pollution harm animals?

Sometimes scientists who study animals (zoologists) and work at zoos help provide places for animals to breed. How does this help to preserve endangered species?

If you were an animal who was a member of an endangered species and you could talk on a TV talk show, what would you say so that people would understand how you felt?

The Prefix **uni** means one, **bi** means two, and **tri** means three. The term cycle refers to wheel. We know that a unicycle refers to a vehicle containing only one wheel; a bicycle is a two-wheeled vehicle, and a tricycle is a three-wheeled vehicle.

■ If **uni** means one, **bi** means two, and **tri** means three, what would the following prefixes mean?

quadra **quint** **sexi** **septi** **octa**

nona **deca**

You're right if you said, four, five, six, seven, eight, nine and ten.

■ Here are some typical bicycle parts. Applying your imagination, knowledge of the prefixes which indicate a number, and the pictures below, use scissors and glue to design, construct, and name a fantastic imaginary vehicle. Good luck!

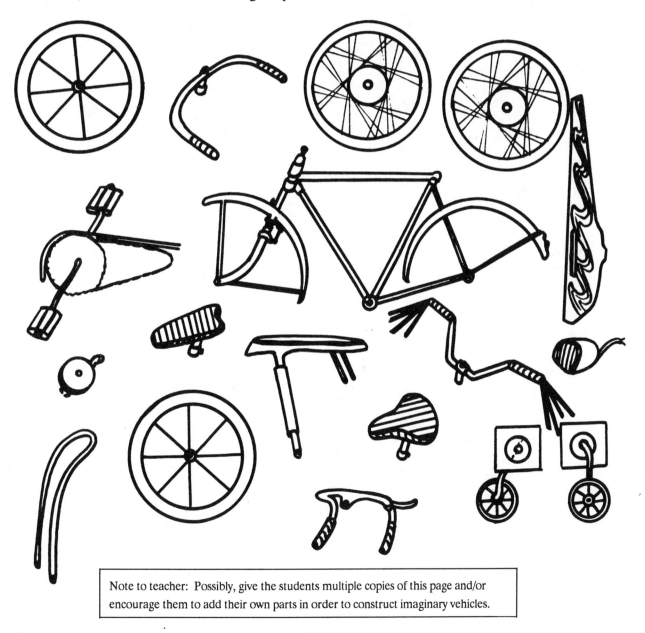

Note to teacher: Possibly, give the students multiple copies of this page and/or encourage them to add their own parts in order to construct imaginary vehicles.

ACROSS

2. A fellow sailor

7. To surround with a circle

9. Toward a later time

10. A figure having three sides and three angles

11. To judge improperly

DOWN

1. Without fear

3. Schoolwork which is done at home

4. To arrange something ahead of time

5. A vehicle having three wheels

6. Having no value or worth

8. To form improperly

ACROSS

3. Within the walls of a building

7. Turning in an upward direction

8. A performer who is outstanding even beyond other star performers

9. Someone who sings ballads

10. To make able

11. To come off of a track

12. An instrument used for transmitting sound (usually voice) over a distance

DOWN

1. Between or among nations

2. To carry something over a distance

4. In a higher direction

5. To manage something improperly

6. To deliver something again

Activity Page: Crossword Puzzle

ACROSS

3. Safe from fire

6. Working together as a team

7. To put into a dangerous situation

8. Smaller than a standard compact item

9. Not correct

DOWN

1. To function improperly

2. Without function or use

3. Something so simple that it can't be damaged, even by a "fool"

4. Canceled at an earlier time

5. A learning setting for children between birth and school age

ACROSS

1. Across the Atlantic Ocean
3. To operate or work at something together
4. Without a place to live
6. To use improperly
7. To read again
9. To handle something improperly
11. To cause something to be tangled
12. Fit for getting pleasure from

DOWN

1. A coded message sent over a distance electronically
2. One who calls for bids at an auction
5. An area smaller than and outside of a city
7. To write again
8. To fail to consent or agree
10. Not faithful or loyal

ACROSS

1. Next to the last or final in a series of events

4. A ship which is operated below the water

6. An amount or number of miles

7. One who takes up space in or occupies a place

9. Between or among states

11. A floor laid below the main floor

DOWN

2. To act or behave improperly

3. The interior or inner part of a body of land

5. To fail to carry out orders

8. Without taste

10. The state of being bored

Activity Page: Crossword Puzzle

ACROSS

1. To raise in value or quality
3. To cause to be closed within an area
5. Across an ocean
7. Not polite
8. Territory which is under rule of a king
10. A vehicle with one wheel
11. To take apart
15. An educational setting where boys and girls learn together
16. Style of dress or costume partially but not fully formal

DOWN

2. Before the season
4. When two separate events occur at the same time
5. A three-legged device for setting up a camera
6. To bring out of a barbaric culture to a civilized culture, to make civil
9. Not perfect
12. To work or operate together
13. Not patient
14. A group smaller and less important than the main group

(page 118)

(page 121)

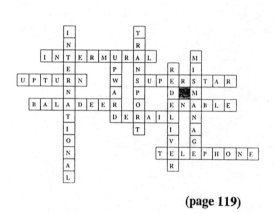

(page 119)

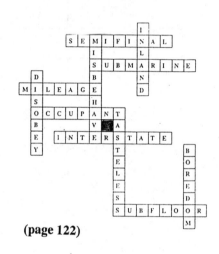

(page 122)

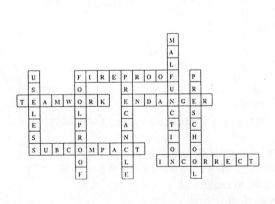

(page 120)

(page 123)